Mistreated

Mistreated

Ron Lee Davis

with
James D. Denney

MULTNOMAH
Portland, Oregon

Unless otherwise indicated, all Scripture references are from the Holy Bible: New International Version, copyright 1973, 1978, 1984, by the International Bible Society. Used by permission of Zondervan Bible Publishers.

Scripture references marked NASB are from the New American Standard Bible, copyright The Lockman Foundation 1960, 1962, 1963, 1968, 1971, 1972, 1973, 1975, 1977. Used by permission.

Scripture references marked RSV are from the Revised Standard Version of the Bible, copyright 1946, 1952, 1971, 1973, Division of Christian Education, National Council of the Churches of Christ in the USA.

Edited by Steve Halliday
Cover design by Bruce DeRoos
Cover Photo by Steve Terrill

MISTREATED
© 1989 Ron Lee Davis and James D. Denney
Published by Multnomah Press
Portland, Oregon 97266

Multnomah Press is a ministry of Multnomah School of the Bible, 8435 N.E. Glisan Street, Portland, Oregon 97220

Printed in the United States of America

Library of Congress Cataloging-in-Publication Data

Davis, Ron Lee.
    Mistreated / Ron Lee Davis.
       p.   cm.
    ISBN 0-88070-325-3
    1. Forgiveness of sins. 2. Cruelty. 3. Resentment. 4. Christian life. I. Title.
BT795.D39   1990
234'.5dc—20   89-29534
                                           CIP

90 91 92 93 94 95 96 97 98 - 10 9 8 7 6 5 4 3 2 1

Dedication

Lovingly dedicated to the people
of the Community Presbyterian Church
of Danville, California,
so many of whom have helped others
to move beyond mistreatment.

Contents

CHAPTER ONE

The First
Step

Janie's family was her greatest pleasure. She had a loving, considerate husband and a cuddly nine-month-old son. She also had the most wonderful father-in-law in the world. Every year, Dad Parker remembered her birthday with a gift of flowers, and could always be counted on for a wink and a generous compliment. His gentle charm and warm smile made him a frequent, welcome visitor in her home.

It was sad that the same could not be said for Dorothy, Janie's mother-in-law. For reasons Janie never understood, Dorothy had never liked her. She had loudly opposed Janie's marriage to her son, and had not spoken a civil word to Janie in the six years since the wedding.

A little before noon on a cold Monday in December, Janie received a phone call with news that Dad Parker had been stricken by a heart attack. She tried to call her husband at work, but he couldn't be reached. So Janie left her baby with a neighbor, got in the car, and rushed to the hospital. She paced anxiously in the elevator as it climbed to the fifth floor. When the doors opened, she rushed down the hall only to be halted at the door of the intensive care unit by her mother-in-law.

"What are *you* doing here?" Dorothy said curtly.

"How is Dad Parker?" Janie asked anxiously, oblivious to the other woman's rudeness.

Dorothy ignored Janie's question. "The doctor is allowing no visitors except family. *You* are not welcome." She glared at Janie for a moment, then turned her back and shut the door, leaving Janie alone in the corridor.

Janie never saw Dad Parker again, for he died that night. To this day, Janie wrestles with anger and resentment toward this hardened, unreasonable woman who treated her so cruelly.

Mistreatment.

Pastor Linden was a man of deep moral conviction. Week by week he stepped into the pulpit and preached from the Scriptures and from his convictions. But some members of his church differed with a few of his convictions. These members didn't go openly to Pastor Linden to talk with him about their differences. They came secretly, by night.

They slit the tires of his car, then climbed over the backyard fence and destroyed the swing set he had built for his daughter. Some time later, Pastor Linden found out who did it, and why. Even after many months had passed, he struggled with resentment toward the church members who had violated the sanctity of his home. "I know I should forgive them," he confided to a close friend, "but I don't know how to turn off this anger I feel."

Mistreatment.

Ruth is a Jewish woman in her forties who converted to Christianity a few years ago. She carries painful memories of growing up in a Protestant neighborhood and experiencing harassment and prejudice for being Jewish. In the grammar school she attended, it was traditional for the children in each class to exchange gifts. One year at the class Christmas party, Ruth was given a brightly colored package to open. She tore off the wrapper and opened the box to find egg shells, orange peels, candy wrappers, empty tuna tins, and crumpled tissues. Garbage. To this day, despite all the years that have passed, Ruth can still taste the humiliation of that experience.

Mistreatment.

Ted is a college student whose father regularly beat and berated him as a child. He has almost no sense of self-worth, a limited ability to focus on his studies, and very little belief in himself or his future. A few years ago, when Ted was in high school, his father lay dying of cancer in a local hospital. Hoping to reconcile, Ted visited his father. They chatted for a few minutes about things like baseball and the weather, then Ted began to say what he had come to say. "I guess I haven't been everything you wanted in a son, Dad," he began, "but I just wanted you to know—"

"That's right," the older man wheezed from his deathbed. "I've been disappointed in you and you've been disappointed in me. Why don't we just leave it that way?" End of discussion. Less than a week later, Ted's father was dead.

Although several years have passed, Ted's voice still chokes with emotion as he asks, "Why couldn't my dad love me?"

Mistreatment.

Mistreatment is one of the painful common denominators of human experience. We all know what it means to be unfairly treated in some arena of our lives—in childhood, in marriage, in our friendships, at school, at church, on the job, and even by society in the form of crime, discrimination, or other kinds of injustice. When abused by a family member, misjudged by a boss, or betrayed by a friend, our first response is, "I don't deserve this! It's not fair!"

And, of course, that's true. Mistreatment is unfair by definition. The word *mistreatment* refers to poor treatment that is undeserved. Most of us try to live a good life, do what's right, and get along with others. Yet, it seems that instead of being rewarded for our efforts, we often suffer more mistreatment. Even worse, it seems that those who do evil actually get ahead in the world.

This doesn't come as news to those familiar with the two-thousand-year-old wisdom of the New Testament, because the apostle Paul has already told us, "Everyone who wants to live a godly life in Christ

Jesus will be persecuted" (2 Timothy 3:12). Or, as Clare Boothe Luce cynically observed, "No good deed goes unpunished."

Mistreatment breaks down our confidence and our sense of self-worth. It fills us with bitter memories and feelings of anger and resentment. We want to get even. Or we want to crawl into a hole and hide. Or we want to forget. But we just can't seem to let go of the hate and the hurt. We can't seem to move beyond our mistreatment.

Sounds bleak, doesn't it? But the good news is that *mistreatment doesn't have to defeat us.* We *can* be healed in our emotions and our self-esteem. The sting can be removed from our painful memories. We can learn how to respond effectively and therapeutically toward those who hurt us. The hurt can be transformed into a positive benefit for our lives, into strength and proven character.

Together, in coming chapters, we will explore practical, workable strategies for:

- healing shattered memories;
- rebuilding broken self-esteem;
- letting go of resentment;
- fully, finally, completely forgiving those who hurt us;
- responding to those who hurt us;
- becoming positive people in a negative world; and
- living free of the tyranny of the past.

I don't pretend that these strategies are fool-proof "handles" for solving your problems, nor am I claiming that the road to emotional freedom will be an easy one. You will need courage, commitment, and honesty along the way. All things worth achieving require serious work, and the achievement of emotional wholeness is no exception. But you are equal to the challenge. I know that because you have the desire to become whole and free. If you didn't, you wouldn't be reading these words right now.

It may be you are a person much like Grace. Not long ago, I received a letter from this dear lady. Grace writes,

Mistreatment entered my life as an unwelcome guest in my childhood. After years of physical and sexual abuse, I left home in my late teens only to enter into a disastrous marriage. My husband's early "social drinking" soon grew to a serious addiction to alcohol. He left me three years ago with two little children to support and nurture. The struggle to balance a full-time job with the duties of a single parent left me feeling lonely, angry and chronically depressed.

Ron, I'm not telling you this because I want you to feel sorry for me. Rather, it's because I want to thank you for the talk you gave last week on mistreatment. It was as though you were speaking directly to me. I'm gradually discovering a whole new freedom from the resentment and bitterness I've carried all these years. In large part because of the encouragement I've received from you, I feel I'm at last beginning to allow God to give me a new life and a new hope.

This letter is typical of many I've received. In over twenty years of speaking and counseling, I've received more response to my talks on mistreatment than on any other subject. For many years, I've been gathering insights into mistreatment from research, personal counseling sessions, and Bible study. The strategy for dealing with mistreatment contained in this book has been tested in the crucible of my own struggle with the hurt of mistreatment, as well as the experience of scores of friends.

You *can* move beyond the hurt of mistreatment. As evidence, I submit the story of Donna, a woman who was radically healed from a trial of extreme mistreatment.

Donna had a home in the suburbs, a generous income from her husband's business, a strong sense of belonging in her church, plus three beautiful children with a fourth on the way. Donna felt she was living a storybook life.

Donna also had a close friend—her best friend from high school, the maid of honor at her wedding, someone with whom she could share any joy, burden, or secret. They talked together on the phone every day. They were present at the births of each other's children. So when this friend and her husband fell upon hard financial times, Donna invited them and their children into her own home for a year so they could save money and get back on their feet.

The arrangement seemed to work well. Then just before her fourth child was born, Donna began to notice a change in her husband, Lee, and in her best friend. Though she tried to deny it, Donna suspected Lee and her friend were having an affair.

Shortly after the baby was born, Donna's life went into a tailspin. The baby came down with mononucleosis, accompanied by high fever and night-long crying. During this period of stress and sleeplessness, Lee told Donna he was leaving.

Donna's storybook world shattered. She withdrew into herself and could no longer care for the baby. She spent her days walking in circles or throwing up in the bathroom. Lee had her committed to the psychiatric ward of a hospital. Then he hired Donna's friend—his lover—to work in his business.

In the hospital, Donna began to gather strength and determination. She decided to fight for her marriage. She talked her way out of the hospital and returned home to care for her children. When she came home, Lee moved out. Day after day, Donna called or visited the office to confront her friend about the affair. During one of these confrontational visits to the office, Lee told Donna, "She and I are planning to get married, and we don't want you to come around here anymore."

That same week, Donna's eldest son came to her with tears in his eyes. "Momma, I want you to shoot me," he said. "This just hurts too much." She hugged him and cried with him and told him God was going to bring their family together again. Throughout the ordeal, which was to last almost three months, Donna prayed several hours each day and sought counseling from her pastor. Her entire church upheld her in prayer.

Finally, those prayers were answered. Lee and Donna's friend broke off the relationship, and she left the office. Lee called Donna and wanted to reconcile. This was what Donna had prayed for—yet she wondered if Lee's repentance was genuine.

Their first night back together was spent at a Christian marriage seminar. As Lee listened to the speakers, read the materials, and went through the communication exercises with Donna, a realization hit him. Amazingly, throughout his affair, Lee never considered how cruelly he had hurt Donna and the children. Though he had once been a loving and considerate husband, his adulterous desire had completely shut off his sensitivity toward his family's feelings. Now, as he sat in the seminar, the shock of what he had done hit him like a sledgehammer.

"After everything I've done to you," he said, weeping in remorse, "I can't believe you still want me as your husband." But she did want him—and she forgave him.

Several weeks later, moved by a compulsion she could not understand, Donna found herself ringing the doorbell of her estranged friend. The door opened and their eyes met—two women who were once best friends, yet who now stood on either side of a deep gulf of hurt. Stunned and momentarily speechless, the other woman invited her in. They talked through the night, recalling fond memories and deep hurts, expressing remorse and forgiveness. By morning, Donna's former friend was a friend again.

The story is not yet over. A marriage that has been so damaged is never mended overnight. It takes time to rebuild broken trust. Donna, Lee, and their children have wounds that only counseling, prayer, and hard work can heal.

But one thing is clear: Though Donna has been to the depths of pain and betrayal, she is moving to a place beyond mistreatment—a place of healing and peace.

I'm firmly convinced it is a place you can reach as well.

CHAPTER TWO

A Quantum Leap

Some years ago, a millionaire—let's call him Mr. Yale—owned a lot in an exclusive residential area of a large city. This lot presented an unusual problem because it was only a couple yards wide by nearly a hundred feet long. Clearly, there was nothing he could do with such an oddly proportioned piece of real estate but sell it to one of the neighbors on either side. So Mr. Yale went first to Mr. Smith, the neighbor on the east side of his lot, and asked if he would be interested in buying it.

"Well," said Mr. Smith, "I really wouldn't have much use for it. But I'll tell you what, since you're in something of a bind, I'd be willing to take it off your hands—purely as a favor, of course." Then he named a ridiculously low price.

"A favor, you say!" Yale exploded. "Why, that's not even one-tenth what the lot is worth!"

"That's all it's worth to me, and that's my offer."

Yale stormed out and went to see the neighbor on the west side, Mr. Jones. To Yale's dismay, Jones bettered the previous offer by only a few dollars. "Look, Yale," Jones said smugly, "I've got you over a barrel and you know it. You can't sell that lot to anyone else and you can't build on it. So there's my offer. Take it or leave it."

"So you think I'm over a barrel?" Yale retorted. "I'll show you no one can cheat me!"

"What are you going to do?"

Yale grinned maliciously. "You just wait!"

Within a few days, the embittered millionaire hired an architect and a contractor to build one of the strangest houses ever conceived. Only five feet wide and running the full length of his property, Yale's house was little more than a row of claustrophobic rooms, each barely able to accommodate a stick of furniture. As the house went up, the neighbors complained that the bizarre structure would blight the neighborhood, but city officials could find no code or regulation to disallow it.

When it was finished, Yale moved into his uncomfortable and impractical house, a self-condemned man in a prison of revenge. There he stayed for many years. Finally, he died there. The house, which became known in the neighborhood as "Spite House," still stands as a monument to one man's hate.

It would be easy to pass judgment on Mr. Yale for making a spectacle of himself, for making himself a prisoner just for the opportunity to get even. Yet I have seen all too many others commit the same self-destructive error. Mr. Yale is neither the first nor the last to imprison himself within walls of resentment and anger.

The bitterness that follows mistreatment often threatens to control us. Our memories are acid-etched with anger, resentment, self-pity. Hate boils in us, filling us with the desire for revenge. Anger turns inward and becomes depression. We know we should forgive. Sometimes we want to forgive. But those bitter feelings keep coming back and we have no control over them. We wonder, "Why can't I shut out the pain, forget the memory, turn off the anger?"

I know those feelings. When I think back on the times I have been unfairly treated, or when I listen to a friend pour out a story of unjust treatment, I'm reminded of the words of God in Isaiah 55:8, "My thoughts are not your thoughts, neither are your ways my ways." I'm often haunted by those words because, according to my ways and my thoughts, if we do right we ought to be rewarded and if we do wrong we ought to be punished. But when we do what is right and are punished for it, we want to cry out, "God, it's not fair!"

God, in his sovereignty, has given human beings free will. If you or I had designed the universe according to our limited insight, we would probably have designed it differently—and free will likely would have been the first thing to go. But in the real universe in which you and I live, there is free will, there is sin, there is mistreatment. Unfair treatment offends our idea of what "ought" to be, so we demand to know, "Why me? Why am I being treated so unfairly?"

Feelings of anger and self-pity in the aftermath of mistreatment are perfectly normal and understandable. But if we fail to move beyond those feelings, we doom ourselves to be enslaved by them.

Our mental, emotional, and spiritual health is on the line. Unless we deliberately choose to relinquish our "right" to wallow in bitterness and self-pity, we may one day awake to find ourselves in an emotional prison that is every bit as real and confining as the wood-and-brick prison of Mr. Yale.

The self-destructive power of bitterness was vividly described by Harry Emerson Fosdick when he said, "Resentment is where you burn down your own house to kill a rat." Fosdick was right. Bitter feelings never cancel out mistreatment. They only further the destruction of a person who already has been hurt.

Hebrews 12:15 warns us against allowing a "root of bitterness" to grow which will poison our souls and defile our relationships with others. In Ephesians 4:31-32, the apostle Paul encourages us, "Get rid of all bitterness, rage and anger, brawling and slander, along with every form of malice. Be kind and compassionate to one another, forgiving each other, just as in Christ God forgave you."

The logical question is *how?* How can I free myself of bitterness, anger, and all the other terrible feelings that haunt me?

The answer begins with a complete shift in your

perspective. Your emotional wholeness depends on your willingness to look at life in a completely new way.

A phrase from the science of physics has passed into our everyday language: "quantum leap." I suspect few people know what a "quantum leap" means to a physicist. Though I'm not a physicist myself, I'm told this term refers to a change in the orbit of an electron around the nucleus of an atom. An electron occupies a certain orbit around the nucleus in line with how much energy it possesses. If an electron attains a higher level of energy, it makes a "quantum leap" from one energy state to another and from one orbit to another—*instantaneously*. The electron doesn't move gradually from one orbit to the next; it simply vanishes from one orbit and appears in the next.

That's the kind of "quantum leap" you and I need to experience in our perspective on mistreatment—a complete re-ordering of our understanding of life. We need to make that instantaneous jump from the old orbit to the new.

For example, many of us have learned to pattern our thinking in completely negative ways. We have fallen under the spell of Murphy's Law, believing that "whatever can go wrong will go wrong." If we get a flat tire on the way to work, if the plumbing backs up in the bathroom, or if we fall on the steps and break an ankle, what is our first response? Usually some variation on "Just my luck!" or "Why do these things always happen to me?"

The good news is that God has repealed Murphy's Law. He has replaced Murphy's Law with grace. By his grace he wants to change our thinking, our outlook, our expectations, and our perspective on our trials of mistreatment. As we allow God to saturate our minds with his grace, we begin to see that the evil things that happen to us can all be woven into God's plan to make us the kind of people he wants us to be. Mistreatment is no longer a meaningless experience of pain that leaves us bitter and twisted. Instead, mistreatment becomes something that enables us to develop new strengths and new levels of understanding.

I think of Larry and Pam, two people who have undergone just this kind of quantum leap in their perspective. Several years ago, when Larry was away on business, a stranger broke into their home. He beat Pam, shoved her into the master bedroom, and raped her on her own bed. Throughout the assault, Pam prayed for the strength to survive. She hoped that once he was through with her, the rapist would leave—and she dared not consider what else he might do. But the man didn't leave. Pam's ordeal continued as he tied her up on the bed, then proceeded to ransack the house. Helplessly she listened as he prowled from room to room, screaming like a madman. "I'm not through, lady!" he raved. "I'm going to take whatever I want from people like you, again and again and again!" She lay in her bonds, her eyes tightly shut, praying he would go away.

Then she heard his footsteps approaching. The footsteps stopped just a few feet away. After a seeming eternity of silence, certain that death was just moments away, Pam opened her eyes. He was still there, but he was not looking at her. He was looking at the wall. She turned her head to see what he was staring at. On the wall above the bed was a portrait of Christ. Arranged on either side of the portrait were several plaques bearing the promises of Christ: "I am with you always." "I am the way and the truth and the life." "Because I live, ye shall live also." "Let not your heart be troubled, neither let it be afraid."

She looked back at the stranger, who stood stock-still, clenching and unclenching his fists. Suddenly a sense of peace washed over her. "Hurting people isn't the answer," she said in a voice surprisingly steady. "The only way you'll ever know peace is to know Jesus Christ."

He looked into her eyes with an unreadable expression. Was he going to leave—or kill her? He looked up again at the portrait of Christ, then left the room. But he didn't leave the house. She could hear him pulling out drawers, dumping valuables onto the floor, overturning furniture.

Minutes passed. The stranger returned again, stopping as before at the foot of the bed. Again he stared at the portrait of Christ. "Where are your car keys?" he asked.

"In my purse," she replied, "on that nightstand."

He went to the nightstand, took the keys, then turned and looked at her. "I came in here to kill you."

Pam nodded. She was ready to die. If only she could tell Larry one last time she loved him—

"But I changed my mind," he continued. "You're a lucky woman. You can thank *him* for saving your life." He thumbed across the room at the portrait. The portrait of Jesus Christ, Pam's Savior.

Then he left.

A few weeks later, the man was captured by police while committing another crime. Larry and Pam received a call from a police lieutenant asking them to come downtown to make an identification. After Pam had identified her assailant and pressed charges against him, she asked if she could talk to him. Surprised, the police lieutenant glanced at Larry. "She knows what she's doing," Larry replied. So they were brought into a small room and seated on one side of a table. The criminal was brought in and seated opposite them while an officer stood by.

Pam and Larry had already prepared themselves for this encounter. Now it was as though God took control, speaking directly through them. "For the first few days after you assaulted me," said Pam in a level voice, "my husband and I hated you. We wanted to hurt you back for what you did to us. But we're all through hating you. We forgive you. The law will hold you accountable for what you've done, but we are not your enemies anymore. We want to tell you why we can forgive you. We want to tell you about the love of Jesus, and how he can take the anger and hate out of your heart."

For about thirty minutes, Larry and Pam talked with this man, telling him about the new life he could discover by giving his life to Christ—and he responded to their Christlike forgiveness. He turned control of his life over to Christ, and the course of his life was reversed.

Yet in those same moments, God was also giving a new life to Larry and Pam. Today they devote their lives to a nationwide prison ministry.

Their experience of mistreatment gives them the authority to speak to thousands of prisoners across the country about the power of God to change hearts, to erase bitterness, and to transform hurt into healing.

What was true for Larry and Pam is true for you and me. The key to emotional wholeness is a new perspective, a new attitude, a new way of looking at life. By God's grace, we can choose a perspective on mistreatment that says, "Whatever happens to me, I expect God to transform it into something good." That was the attitude of Paul, who wrote in 2 Corinthians 4:8-9, "We are hard pressed on every side, but not crushed; perplexed, but not in despair; persecuted, but not abandoned; struck down, but not destroyed." Paul knew what he was talking about. He endured more mistreatment in an average year than most people face in a lifetime: riots, beatings, stonings, imprisonment, plots against his life, slander, and opposition of every conceivable kind. Yet, as he wrote in Romans 8:28 (NASB), he believed that "God causes all things to work together for good to those who love God, to those who are called according to His purpose."

The common perspective on mistreatment is "It's not fair! I can't accept this! I'll never forget how I was hurt! No one gets away with doing that to me! I have a right to get even!"

The new perspective on mistreatment which leads to emotional wholeness says, "I understand that injustice and mistreatment are a part of life. I can't always control what others do to me, but I can control how I will respond to them. I choose to forgive. I choose to get on with my life. I trust the fact that God can take all the circumstances of my life, even the painful circumstances of mistreatment, and weave them together in a pattern that brings about good in my own life and in the lives of others around me."

During the writing of this book, I made a trip to Africa where I met a woman named Zodie. She taught me a lot about perspective in a crisis of mistreatment. Zodie is an Ethiopian Christian nurse who accompanied me and several American companions, showing us the work being done to meet the medical, nutritional, and spiritual needs of the Ethiopian people.

A year before I met Zodie, however, she was in prison. Her "crime," according to Ethiopia's Marxist government, was her Christian faith. She and a number of other Christians had gathered to sing hymns, pray, and worship God. Suddenly the little one-room house in which they met was invaded by hard-faced men with weapons. Zodie and her companions were dragged out of the village and thrown into prison without trial. During their imprisonment, Zodie and her fellow Christians were cursed, beaten, interrogated at midnight, and offered "meals" consisting of things you and I would not recognize as food.

The men were kept in one primitive cell, the women in another. There were no beds. Everyone slept on the dirt floor. In each cell, the Christian prisoners paired up so they could take turns sleeping. Why sleep in shifts? Because nighttime brought out a particularly vicious African tick that burrows into the flesh and transmits diseases. For three hours, one person would watch for crawling parasites and remove them from his or her sleeping friend. At the end of three hours, the sleeper would watch and the watcher would sleep. It was a beautiful demonstration of practical love and caring.

Zodie told me many other stories of her imprisonment as well. I was amazed by the simple, matter-of-fact way she related the most harrowing and revolting circumstances she and other African Christians had endured. Finally I said to her, "It must have been very hard for you to survive those months in prison."

"Oh, no!" she said, her face beaming. "No, Ron, it was just so sweet to know I was in prison for Jesus." What a perspective to have in a crisis of mistreatment!

But a new perspective is just the beginning of the healing process. Somehow, we have to find ways to cleanse ourselves, fully and finally, of all those poisonous, painful feelings. We have to find a way to mend those broken memories. We have to find a way out of the role of *victim of* mistreatment and into the role of *victor over* mistreatment.

And that is what we shall learn next.

CHAPTER THREE

You Are Not
a Victim

Lauren met Greg at the university where she was majoring in the humanities. He was premed. Soon they fell in love and were married. They agreed on a plan whereby Lauren would set aside her studies for the next several years and would work two jobs—sixty hours a week—to support them while Greg continued his studies. Later, when Greg had completed his courses and was making a living as a doctor, it would be Lauren's turn to go back to school and get her degree.

For six years following their marriage, Lauren loved and encouraged Greg while supporting him financially. She deferred her education, her social life, and her desire for children so that she and Greg could build their dream.

Today, Greg is a doctor with a successful practice . . . a thousand miles from where Lauren lives alone in a small apartment. Even before obtaining his M.D. degree, he was having an affair with another woman and planning to take her with him to another state, where—without telling Lauren—he had arranged to serve his internship.

Lauren is divorced and saddled with debt from their broken marriage. She can't afford to return to school and can't force Greg to pay her the court-ordered divorce settlement even though he now has a six-figure annual income. Lauren is bitter, trapped by feelings of anger and betrayal. Though she wants to put Greg behind her, she finds every hour is a struggle against an all-consuming hatred. She sees herself as a victim of Greg's mistreatment.

Scott has served as a Sunday school teacher and an elder in his church. A small group in the church differs from Scott on a number of issues. One of these people heard a derogatory rumor about Scott. Without bothering to check the facts or to ask Scott about it, this man gleefully seized the opportunity to discredit Scott by spreading the rumor to others. The story was false, but the damage to Scott's reputation is done. Today Scott feels like an outcast in the church he helped build. He attends services rarely and feels depressed and resentful when he does attend, having to sit across the aisle from those who have treated him so callously. Scott sees himself as a victim of mistreatment.

Janet's husband, a successful businessman, is continually on the road. As he travels from city to city, he is involved in one casual affair after another with women he meets in his business, in bars, and even with prostitutes. He has openly disclosed his adulterous lifestyle to his wife. "This is what I enjoy," he told her, "and I'm not going to change, so you can either leave me or get used to it. It's up to you." Though Janet has faithfully tried to serve God throughout her life, she now finds herself cruelly mistreated by the man she married. She both loves and hates this man and doesn't know what to do. She feels trapped, a victim of her husband's mistreatment.

These stories all demonstrate how injustice functions in this unfair world. Lauren, Scott, and Janet are good, caring, conscientious people who have tried to live upright lives. In return, they have been betrayed or slandered or used and tossed aside. They have been cast in the role of victims and unless they find a way to escape that role, the hurt that was done to them once in their lives will continue to hurt them again and again.

As we saw in chapter 2, a crucial first step in moving ourselves out of the victim role is a complete reordering of our perspective. We have to move beyond our naive expectation that if we do good, things will turn out all right. Our perception must expand to embrace the fact that the good we do will sometimes be punished, not rewarded; that the person who tells the truth will sometimes be scorned as a liar; that the person who deals out gentleness and understanding will often be paid back in anger and hatred. That's the world we live in. To pretend otherwise is to set ourselves up for deep disappointment, disillusionment, and depression.

My friend Robert understands the world's unfairness. Now retired, he was an officer in a savings and loan branch in southern California. His boss was George, the branch manager. What Robert didn't know during the two years he and George worked together was that George was embezzling from the company—and that he was secretly setting up Robert to "take the rap."

Auditors caught up with George before he could complete his scheme. Even so, he had succeeded in stealing over $200,000—and he had placed a number of false, derogatory reports in Robert's personnel file as part of his plan to frame Robert. George was fired from the savings and loan, and was required to make restitution, which he was allowed to pay in installments over four years. He received a suspended sentence. Then he got a new job with a public relations firm at an *increase* in salary. The end result of George's theft scarcely amounted to a slap on the wrist.

And what happened to honest, diligent, hardworking Robert? The false information George had planted in his personnel file was never removed— "company policy," he was told. Robert was denied promotions for the next six years. His career was stuck in neutral while the confessed thief was given a higher paying job. Is that fair? Of course not. But that's the way this world often works.

Yet Robert refused to accept the role of victim. He continued giving the company 100 percent of his effort until he retired. "Sure, I could be bitter about what happened," he says today, "but what good would that do? I chose to hang in with the company, partly out of pragmatism—I wanted to protect my pension. But it goes deeper than that. Some people might say I was just being a doormat. But in my heart, I know the reason I stayed on the job was not because I was a wimp. I stayed because I'm too tough to be beaten by unfair treatment. I've got a lot of friends on the job, both co-workers and customers, and I feel I have a positive effect on the people I see every day. More than that, my job is not my whole life. My life is a lot bigger than those knocks I've taken at the office, and I'm not going to let it get me down."

Clearly, this is not the perspective of a "victim."

How can you and I respond to mistreatment without falling into the victim role? First, we need to understand that there are invisible emotional and relational ties between ourselves and the people who mistreat us. Those ties are like the control wires of a marionette. We may not be aware of them, but they are there all the same—and the task before us, as we seek to become emotionally whole and liberated, is to cut those invisible control wires.

As long as we harbor bitterness toward the person who has hurt us, we allow that person to control and victimize us. We may be carrying the memories of some mistreatment that happened ten, twenty, or thirty years ago, and the person who hurt us may even be dead and buried—but as long as we clutch the bitterness of that mistreatment, we continue to be negatively, emotionally bound to those who hurt us. They continue to pull our strings and push our buttons, to control our emotions and our responses—but only if we let them.

You don't have to remain a victim. You can move to a place where you are free of other people's damaging control. Someone may have hurt you back then, but this is now. The old events that continue to play and replay in your mind can be turned off.

You may say, "You don't know how deeply I've been hurt. After what was done to me, I can never forgive Person X." Person X may be a parent, a friend, a co-worker, or a stranger. His or her offense against you may be anything from a single insult to a childhood full of destructive abuse. Whatever the offense, the underlying principle is the same: As long as you hold on to your bitterness, you continue to be a victim. What you are really saying is that this person victimized you in the past, continues to victimize you now, and there is nothing you will ever be able to do about it. You have accepted the victim role.

My reply? Yes, you were deeply hurt back then and there is nothing you can do to change the past. But you can change what you do *now.* That means a perspective change. That means work and commitment on your part. It means you refuse to accept the role of victim. You determine to wrest control of your feelings from that abuser and you now choose to take responsibility for your own feelings and your own responses to life.

When a child is mistreated or abused, he or she is powerless, an innocent victim. But an adult has some say over how the past will penetrate and affect the present. An adult has the power to throw off the role of "victim." When we are mistreated, you and I have a choice either to accept the reality of injustice in an unjust world and get on with our lives, or to simply accept the bitter role of victim.

When I think of someone who endured enormous mistreatment, yet who refused to accept the victim role, I think of a young man named Joseph whose story is told in the Old Testament book of Genesis. Most people are familiar with the story of Joseph and his famous coat, of how he was sold into slavery by his brothers and how he eventually became the right-hand man of Pharaoh.

But Joseph's story is much more than just an interesting tale from an ancient time. His life resonates with the same hurts that face us at the end of the twentieth century. If you have ever been mistreated by a family member, if you've ever been falsely accused, if you've been misjudged and unfairly treated by an employer, if you've ever been abandoned by a friend—then you have a lot in common with Joseph.

Joseph's story begins in Genesis 37. We meet him as a seventeen-year-old youth, embroiled in family turmoil. Joseph's father Jacob indulged him as the favorite son, treating him to a pampered lifestyle symbolized by the gift of a richly ornamented robe. Joseph's ten older brothers, by contrast, were treated like hired hands. They deeply resented their father's favoritism toward Joseph and their resentment was stoked all the more when Joseph told them of his dreams—dreams which portrayed his brothers as bowing down before him.

One day, far from their father's home, the brothers seized Joseph and threw him down a dry well. At first planning to kill him, finally they thought it more profitable to sell him to Arab traders for cash. Thus, Joseph was sold into slavery—and so began his lengthy trial of mistreatment.

Note that in the beginning it was not so much Joseph as his brothers who suffered the sting of parental mistreatment. Jacob heartlessly flaunted his favoritism toward Joseph. The brothers simply took the mistreatment they received from Jacob and the resentment they felt toward Jacob and laid it all upon Joseph. They tore Joseph's′ beautiful coat—the symbol of their father's unfairness—and dipped it in the blood of an animal. Then they took it back to Jacob with a lie about how Joseph died in the jaws of some wild animal.

Imagine the angry, bitter thoughts that must have gone through the minds of these young men as they watched their father grieve over his favorite son: *We needed a father, but you never treated us like sons! You never gave us your love and approval! You were never involved in our problems! You deprived us of a father's love! Well, now we've deprived you of a son!* Like so many negligent, absent, or unjust fathers in our own time, Jacob allowed destructive dynamics to grow under his own roof and as a result reaped a harvest of sorrow.

Joseph, meanwhile, was taken in chains to Egypt, where he was sold to a nobleman named Potiphar. There he proved himself so valuable to his employer that he was placed in charge of the entire household. Unfortunately, Potiphar's wife also took an interest in Joseph. In fact, she used every means at her disposal to seduce him, engaging in what in today's workplace we would call "sexual harassment." Joseph resisted her advances, even though she tempted, cajoled, and pressured him day after day. Finally, unable to break the resolve and integrity of Joseph, she slandered him, accusing him of attempted rape.

How easy it is to identify with Joseph at this point! There are few things in life we guard so jealously as our reputation. Here, Joseph's reputation is being trashed as well as his career as the captain of Potiphar's household. How would you or I face such outrageous accusations from the boss's wife? Certainly, we would want to defend ourselves: "It's a lie! It's not fair! How can I set the record straight?"

Yet, all too often in this life, there is no way to set the record straight. Sometimes the lie stands and we fall. That's what Joseph found out. Potiphar believed his wife's lie, misjudged his faithful servant Joseph, and had Joseph thrown into prison.

Though I don't claim to have suffered anything like the intense mistreatment Joseph endured, I can identify with him and learn from him. There have been times, in both my private life and my public ministry, when I have felt misunderstood, misjudged, and falsely accused. Again and again, I've gone back to a little booklet called *Seven Secrets to Spiritual Power*, written by A. W. Tozer. One of Tozer's seven secrets is this: "Never defend yourself." Yes, we defend people who have no one else to defend them. Yes, we do what we can to clarify communication, to correct misunderstandings. But we will never move out of the victim role until we stop being defensive.

Healing from the hurt of slander and unjust accusation comes when we realize (and this will be a quantum shift for most of us) that because we have been justified by the work of Jesus Christ on the cross, we no longer need to justify ourselves. As Paul writes in Romans 3:24, you and I "are justified freely by his grace through the redemption that came by Christ Jesus." We do not need to defend ourselves because God is our defense.

That is one of the powerful lessons of Joseph's life: God was his defense. Yes, he endured mistreatment. Yes, he was falsely accused. And yes, he was falsely imprisoned. Yet throughout Joseph's story in the last fourteen chapters of Genesis, through the darkest moments of his trial of slavery and imprisonment, we see the words, "The LORD was with Joseph." God was present with Joseph, working out the details of his story, bringing good out of all the evil that had been done to him.

While in prison, Joseph did a favor for Pharaoh's chief butler, who had been imprisoned some time before for having displeased the king. As the chief butler was about to be released, Joseph asked him to remember the favor and so to secure Joseph's own release from prison. The chief butler promised to remember—but failed to keep his promise. Joseph languished behind bars for two more years, abandoned and forgotten by his friend.

Please remember that Joseph was a flesh-and-blood human being like ourselves, wounded by a hurt that came not from an enemy, but from someone trusted and counted on, someone considered a friend. You may know the sting of having a friend abandon you, betray you, or break a confidence. It cuts deeply, doesn't it?

Throughout Joseph's story, we see a young man enduring trial after trial of mistreatment, seemingly every kind of injustice one could face. Yet—and this is a key lesson—we never see Joseph surrender to the role of "victim." I've read Joseph's story in every Bible translation I can find, and I've never found even a hint of bitterness or self-pity in his spirit. He simply refused to let mistreatment defeat him.

Joseph was thirty years old when he finally emerged from prison. From the time he was sold into slavery until his release from that Egyptian dungeon, he had endured thirteen years of injustice. But Joseph did not merely while away those long, painful years. He used that time to develop a winsome and charming demeanor, a keen intellect, a godly temperament, and a spiritual gift of wisdom. When he came out of prison and was brought before Pharaoh, Pharaoh recognized these special qualities in Joseph's speech, in his bearing, in his visionary insight. So Pharaoh elevated this wise young man to the position of prime minister, second-in-charge over all Egypt.

At the end of Genesis, Joseph is reunited with his brothers. At last he has the opportunity and the power to exact his long-delayed revenge against the brothers who had sold him into slavery. But Joseph doesn't want revenge. He just wants a whole relationship with his family. Joseph forgives his brothers, embraces them, and weeps over them.

As I look at this man's life and compare my own trials of mistreatment with his, I am in awe. *What a way to live!* I think. I want to have the kind of character Joseph had. I want to see my trials of mistreatment transformed into proven character and a positive influence on those around me.

Joseph made some right choices during some wrong experiences in his life. And I don't simply refer here to the right moral choices. His choices were *therapeutically* the right choices for his spiritual, emotional, mental, and physical health. He rejected resentment and bitterness. He rejected revenge. He rejected the role of victim. So can you and I.

In the 1930s, a prison was built on a sunny tropical paradise called Cuba. The capacity of Isla de Piños Prison so far exceeded the needs of the country that many people wondered, "Who will fill the prison?" In the late 1950s, a new dictator named Castro came into power, and he quickly packed the prison to more than its capacity. Of those prisoners—most of whom were arrested purely because of their political opinions—one was twenty-three-year-old Armando Valladares. He remained in Isla de Piños until an international campaign of protest finally secured his release at age forty-five.

Executions were staged each night during Valladares's first year in prison. Armed guards entered the cell block after midnight, cursing and rousting selected prisoners out of bed. The doomed men were dragged into the yard under the view of the cell windows. The prisoners in the cells watched as their friends were trussed to wooden stakes and shot. Many of the prisoners were devout Christians who had been imprisoned simply because the atheistic Castro regime felt threatened by men of religious conviction. As these Christians went to their deaths, they shouted, *"Viva Cristo Rey!"* "Long live Christ the King!" Prison officials found these cries of faith so disturbing that they ordered the condemned men gagged for execution.

In his memoirs, *Against All Hope*, Valladares later wrote,

> When I heard the discharges of the rifles, I would be seized with horror, and I embraced Christ in desperation. I had come to prison with some religious feeling; my beliefs were genuine but no doubt superficial at that time, since they had never been submitted to hard trial. . . .

> There came a moment when, seeing those young men full of courage depart to die before the firing squad and shout "Viva Cristo Rey!" at the fateful instant, I not only understood instantly, as though by a sudden revelation, that Christ was indeed there for me at the moments when I prayed not to be killed, but realized as well that He served to give my life, and my death if it came to that, ethical meaning. . . .
> It was at that moment, I am sure, that Christianity became, more than a religious faith, a way of life for me. Because of my situation, it seemed my life would necessarily be a life of resistance, but I would be sustained in it by a soul filled with love and hope.[1]

Sustained over the next two decades by the love and hope of his newly tempered and tested faith, Valladares endured some of the most vile and sadistic tortures imaginable. At one time, he was placed in solitary confinement for several months. He was shut up in a small concrete cell with no bed, no shower, and no basin. The toilet was a hole in the floor. The iron door of the cell was welded shut. The top of the cell was covered with wire mesh and the prison guards walked along a catwalk above the cells, poking so-called "Ho Chi Minh poles" through the mesh to prod the prisoners whenever they began to sleep. The guards changed shifts every six hours, and Valladares seldom got more than a few consecutive minutes of sleep during his months in solitary confinement. Several times, a sadistic guard dumped a five-gallon pail of human waste on him, which dried in his hair and on his body. Often when his meager rations were slid under the door, he found that someone had contaminated the already-loathsome food with kerosene.

Valladares later recalled,

> The lack of sleep and the tension were seriously affecting me. I sought God then. . . . I never asked Him to get me out of there. I didn't think that God should be used for that kind of request. I only asked that He allow me to resist, that He give me the faith and spiritual strength to bear up under these conditions without sickening with hatred. I only prayed for Him to accompany me. And His presence, which I felt, made my faith an indestructible shield.[2]

On another occasion, Valladares and a number of other prisoners were marched barefoot, clad only in underwear, over sharp, coral-like rocks which the Cubans call "dog's teeth." The prisoners' feet, knees, and hands were cruelly shredded as they stumbled over these rocks. But the worst was still to come. The prisoners were shoved, despite their bleeding wounds, into a ditch which carried raw sewage from the prison to a holding pond. As the guards prodded and beat the men with poles, the prisoners were forced along that ditch, sometimes stumbling into filth so deep it covered their heads. For weeks afterwards, Valladares and his companions were afflicted with eye infections, hepatitis, and digestive disorders. One man's eardrum was destroyed by infection.

Prisoners were shot, beaten, burned, hacked by machetes, asphyxiated, emasculated, bayoneted, and subjected to biological experiments. Yet, even as the ferocity of the prison officials intensified, the will and resistance of the prisoners grew stronger. Valladares and his fellow prisoners engaged in peaceful protests, hunger strikes, work stoppages. When the political commissioner of the prison asked Valladares where the prisoners got the strength to go on in the face of hunger and torture, he replied, "We have an inexhaustible supply of strength, sir, an imperishable source called love."

Though it ranked among the most monstrous places in history, the Isla de Piños Prison became a place of Christian revival, a place where Christian love and courage grew to their most sublime. Throughout his ordeal, Armando Valladares kept before him the image of another tortured, dying, bleeding man—a man upon a wooden cross who prayed for his executioners, "Father, forgive them, for they know not what they do." When Valladares walked out of that place, he left without hatred, without bitterness—but with a powerful story to tell. Like Joseph, Valladares used his prison time to grow deeper in faith, stronger in courage, richer in Christian love. And like Joseph, Valladares rejected the role of "victim."

That is the choice you and I must make before we can proceed to the next stage of our emotional healing. Like the electron which exchanges the old energy state for the new and which instantaneously leaps from one orbit to the next, you and I can make that "quantum leap" in our self-image. By God's grace, we can choose to reject the image of ourselves as victims of mistreatment. We can begin to see ourselves—not by some trick of wishful thinking, but with bold confidence—as victors over mistreatment.

Believe this: You *are* a victor over mistreatment. For that—as coming chapters will unfold—is the promise and the future God is already working out within you.

Notes

1. Armando Valladares, *Against All Hope* (New York: Ballantine Books, 1987), pp. 18-19.

2. Ibid., p. 176.

CHAPTER FOUR

The 50:20
Principle

A true story, believe it or not, as told in Bellamy Partridge's 1939 book *Country Lawyer.*

It had been a dry summer for a small town in upstate New York, circa 1885. Wells were drying up. Crops were wilting on surrounding farms. But the new Presbyterian minister in town, a young man named Duncan McLeod, had an idea: prayer. He had leaflets printed, encouraging everyone in and around the town to pause at a designated time and pray for rain. Scores of the faithful from his church went door to door, handing out the leaflets at homes, shops, and even saloons and poolhalls. Every person in town, regardless of creed or church affiliation, was invited to join the prayer. The response of the town was unanimous and enthusiastic, with one exception—a curmudgeonly old farmer named Phineas Dodd.

Farmer Dodd stormed over to Rev. McLeod's house with one of the leaflets in hand and pounded on the door. When the minister answered the door, Dodd waved the leaflet under his nose and demanded, "What kind of foolishness is this?! Just who do you think you are, meddling in the affairs of the Almighty?! The Lord will send a drenching rain or withering blast as he chooses, and it's not for the likes of you to be trying to change the Lord's mind for him!" Before the minister could reply, Dodd turned and stamped off.

The next day—a particularly hot August Saturday—was the appointed day, and noon was the appointed hour. All the townspeople set aside their knitting needles, hammers, butcher knives, or pool cues, and raised their hands in prayer. All the town's business came to a halt for five minutes. At the end of that time, everyone waited and watched the sky.

An hour passed. Clouds appeared. Two hours. A gusty wind arose. Three hours. The temperature dropped twenty degrees; thunderheads formed aloft. Four hours after the prayer, the streets were awash in water, and the outlying fields were drenched. Oh, and one more thing happened: Lightning struck the hay barn of Phineas Dodd and promptly burned it to the ground.

On Sunday, church attendance swelled phenomenally as the townspeople crowded into the sanctuary to thank God and congratulate Rev.

McLeod on his idea. On Monday, however, Farmer Dodd was seen charging through the muddy town streets to the courthouse. There he filed suit against the Presbyterian Church and Rev. McLeod, seeking five thousand dollars in damages for his ruined barn.

As the young minister nervously entered the courtroom on the first day of the trial, Dodd glared icily and said, "Ah, there he is—the smart young man who calls down rain and burns down the barns of hard-working farmers! I told you not to meddle in the ways of the Almighty, didn't I? Well, I'll get even with you!" The trial commenced, and for the first two days Dodd's attorney presented witness after witness to prove that Rev. McLeod had organized the community prayer and had received congratulations for its success.

After Dodd himself testified, the church's attorney, Samuel Partridge, cross-examined. "Mr. Dodd, how long is it since you prayed?"

"Don't recollect."

"Do you believe in the power of prayer?"

"No . . . I mean, yes . . . I mean, some prayers work, some don't. But that prayer that Rev. McLeod thought up—well, that was no ordinary prayer! He got the whole town to back him! And the storm blew up the very same afternoon they did their praying!"

"Didn't that storm cover half the state of New York?"

"I don't care if that storm blew from here to Brazil! I only care about one barn that burned to the ground because that preacher called down a storm from heaven!"

The trial lasted three days. At the conclusion of the trial, the judge determined that Rev. McLeod and the townspeople had prayed only for rain, not lightning. The bolt that destroyed the barn was an act of God for which neither Rev. McLeod nor the Presbyterian Church could be held liable. He banged his gavel and said, "I find for the defendants. The plaintiff, Phineas Dodd, is ordered to pay court costs."

Dodd jumped up and turned to the minister. "I'm not through with you yet! I'll get even! You'll see! I'll take this to a higher court!" But Farmer Dodd never carried out his threat to "get even" in a higher court. That autumn, he was so busy harvesting the record-yield crops on his lush, rain-blessed acreage that he never got around to filing an appeal.

Like Farmer Dodd, people bearing grudges often make spectacles of themselves. Bitterness distorts judgment, blinding people to their own best interests. Throughout history, the lust to "get even" has driven people to astronomical heights of foolishness. One bizarre example is that of the notorious Roman emperor Caligula.

As a young man, Caligula desperately coveted the Roman throne, even though his uncle Tiberius was then king and Caligula was outside the line of succession. Young Caligula consulted a fortune-teller, demanding a prophecy that he would one day rule the empire. The old crone looked the youth up and down, then asked a gold coin in advance. When he had paid, she said to him with a sneer, "The spirits say only this of your future: You can no more be emperor than you can ride a horse across the Bay of Naples. Now, get away from me, you arrogant pup!"

"You'll regret your insolence!" shouted Caligula as he stamped away. "I'll have you boiled alive when I'm emperor!"

Caligula never forgot his grudge against the fortune-teller. Over the next few years, he orchestrated the removal—by political maneuvering and murder—of those who barred his way to the throne. Finally, Caligula was crowned emperor, and one of his first official acts was to send troops into the streets of the city to find the fortune-teller who had prophesied his failure. The soldiers returned with word that the fortune-teller had died several years earlier.

Denied his revenge, Caligula raved and bellowed in frustration. Then an idea struck him: "If I cannot avenge myself against that old seer's living flesh, I'll avenge myself against her ghost! When I disprove the rest of the prophecy, the old crone's spirit will hear of it even in the abyss!"

So Caligula set about to prove he could ride a horse across the Bay of Naples, a six-mile-wide expanse of water. He ordered harbormasters from throughout Italy and Sicily to detain all vessels, confiscate their cargo, and send the ships to the Bay of Naples. About three thousand ships were collected this way, but it was still not enough, so Caligula ordered another one thousand ships built especially for his mad scheme. The ships were anchored side by side and lashed together in a line that stretched from the docks of Puteoli to Caligula's villa at Bauli. The decks were covered with dirt which was packed down to form a road. More ships were added, forming island-like villages at selected points along the way.

When all was prepared to his satisfaction, Caligula donned his jewel-embroidered cloak and performed a ceremony in which he declared himself a god. Then, leading a two-hundred-horse cavalry and a twenty-thousand-man infantry, Caligula set out on horseback from his villa and crossed the floating road that spanned the Bay of Naples. Arriving at Puteoli, he launched a festival of drinking, rioting, and looting that nearly destroyed the town. Caligula spurred his horse along the docks, careless of innocent lives. Over three hundred men, women, and children were either trampled or knocked into the Bay and drowned. To cap off the entertainment, Caligula ordered his own imperial flagship rammed and sunk; its bewildered crew was drowned.

The rioting lasted two days. The event completely drained the imperial treasury. A few weeks later, at the urging of his advisors, Caligula reluctantly ordered the ships returned to their owners— but it was too late. Before the order could be implemented, a heavy storm churned across the Bay of Naples and sank half the ships of the floating road. The loss of ships caused a shortage of vessels which had been used to import grain from Egypt. Over the next few years, thousands throughout the Italian peninsula died in the famine that resulted from Caligula's irrational grudge against a dead fortune-teller.

Resentment often inspires a kind of diabolic creativity, resulting in cunning forms of revenge. The empress Josephine, wife of Napoleon, once planned a gala reception at her chateau at Malmaison. A friend informed Josephine that one of the invited guests—a social rival whom Josephine detested and with whom she continually competed—had purchased a deep green dress especially for the occasion. She had specifically chosen the deep green color, Josephine's friend explained, to contrast stunningly with the ivory and silver furnishings of Josephine's drawing room. Josephine immediately went to work, sparing no expense to have the room hastily redecorated. New wallpaper, drapery, rugs, and furniture were purchased—all in a striking shade of blue designed to make Josephine's rival appear vulgar and gaudy in her green dress.

A glance at our own century reveals that the art of creative vindictiveness has not been lost. One customer of the Bank of Marin, located in an affluent suburb north of San Francisco, carried out his revenge with a distinctly Californian flair. Like all banks, the Bank of Marin offers a standard assortment of so-called "scenic checks" featuring idyllic backgrounds of wildflowers, sunsets, or mountain streams. But this bank also pioneered an innovation: personalized scenic checks. For an extra fee, customers could bring in a favorite photo of themselves, their children, or the family dog and have it printed on their checks. One man bought a special set of personalized checks to be used only for making his alimony payments. These checks featured a picture of the man in a passionate embrace . . . with his new wife!

Undeniably, this man came up with an inventive approach to getting even with his "ex." An inventive, vindictive, hateful, hurtful approach. All of these people—Farmer Dodd, Caligula, Josephine, and the California man with his special checks— were driven to strange and costly forms of behavior in their quest for revenge. But before we pass judgment on these people, we should remember that the same vindictive spirit lives in you and me. We're just a little more subtle about it.

Revenge is one of the oldest of human impulses, dating back to the day Cain murdered Abel. The poet Byron wrote of "the sweetness of revenge." The brooding philosopher Nietzsche called revenge "the greatest instinct of the human race." Francis Bacon called revenge "a wild justice."

When we are mistreated, it is only natural that we want to fight back, to get even. That's a basic instinct in the human species. But God wants us to move beyond mere animal response. The image of God was stamped upon us at creation, was broken by sin, and is now being restored in us as God seeks to conform us (as Romans 8:28-29 tells us) into the image of Christ. And the image God has given us in the example of his Son Jesus is an image of forgiveness and mercy, not revenge.

Martin Luther King, Jr., once observed, "Jesus knew that the old eye-for-an-eye philosophy would leave everyone blind. He did not seek to overcome evil with evil. He overcame evil with good. Although crucified by hate, he responded with aggressive love." The prevailing view of this world is, "Why should I let anyone get away with mistreating me—and then forgive him just as if nothing ever happened? He hurt me! I have a right to pay him back!" But because Jesus came and taught us the depth and breadth of God's forgiveness by dying on the cross, our attitude must be, "I owe the world a debt of forgiveness, because I have been freely forgiven by God." We may not deserve to be mistreated, and our offender may not deserve to be forgiven—but when we forgive, we counterbalance the other person's sin with the grace of God.

Turning again to Genesis and the life of Joseph, we find a powerful example of what it means to live a life of grace and forgiveness. Joseph was sold into slavery by his brothers, slandered by his employer's wife, misjudged by his employer, falsely imprisoned and abandoned by a friend—yet without bitterness, without a hint of vengefulness. Joseph would have affirmed the words of Frederick Buechner, "To lick your wounds, to smack your lips over grievances long past, to roll over your tongue the prospect of bitter confrontations still to come, to savor to the last toothsome morsel both the pain you are given and the pain you are giving back—in many ways it is a feast fit for a king. The chief drawback is that what you are wolfing down is yourself. The skeleton at the feast is you."[1]

Joseph refused to be consumed by bitterness. He forgave and he trusted himself to God. And toward the end of his story, when he was reunited with those who set in motion his thirteen-year trial of mistreatment, Joseph responded by forgiving and accepting his brothers. He did not forgive like you and I so often do, by saying, "I guess I have to forgive you—but I really can't forget what you did. From now on, there will be distance between you and me."

No, Joseph fully and completely forgave his brothers. He drew them close to himself, embraced them, and wept over them. Yet the reality of such unconditional forgiveness completely escaped the brothers' comprehension. For years after Joseph forgave and reconciled with his brothers, the guilt of their sin continued to gnaw at their consciences. They were afraid that his forgiveness was just an act, that someday Joseph, using his almost limitless power as the prime minister of Egypt, would finally take his long-delayed revenge against them.

The inner workings of Joseph's heart remained totally mysterious to the brothers. How, they wondered, could a man suffer the kind of mistreatment we inflicted on him and not hunger for revenge? Their ignorance of Joseph's forgiving heart filled them with fear—the fear of punishment. Genesis 50 records that, following the death of their father Jacob, the brothers' guilt and fear grew so great that they threw themselves at Joseph's feet and begged him to accept them—not as brothers but as slaves.

What a temptation it would be to possess absolute power over the person who once mistreated you! Joseph had that kind of absolute power. If you had been in Joseph's place, how would you have handled his power?

Often when we are mistreated, we are tempted to use guilt to manipulate others. If Joseph had been a guilt-manipulator, he might have said, "You know, brothers, when Dad was alive, you made life pretty miserable for him. Remember what you did after you sold me into slavery? You told Dad I'd been killed by an animal. You let him live in torment with the lie that I was dead." But Joseph refused to seek revenge by guilt-manipulation.

What did Joseph do when he saw the guilt and fear on his brothers' faces? Genesis 50:17 says that

Joseph wept. Why? Because his brothers didn't understand his heart. They couldn't comprehend the genuineness of his words, "I love you, I forgive you, I want to be close to you." They were incapable of receiving authentic forgiveness and grace. That was a tragedy that broke the heart of Joseph.

So Joseph gave his brothers a beautiful gift—the gift of unexpected grace. Genesis 50:19-21, three of the most beautiful verses in the entire Old Testament, paint a moving, captivating picture of Christlike grace and unconditional love: "But Joseph said to them, 'Don't be afraid. Am I in the place of God? You intended to harm me, but God intended it for good. . . . So then, don't be afraid. I will provide for you and your children.' And he reassured them and spoke kindly to them."

The heart of these verses is what I call "the 50:20 Principle," so called because it comes from Genesis 50:20 (RSV): "You meant evil against me; but God meant it for good." This is a beautiful expression of Christlike grace and it's found not in the New Testament, but in the first book of the Old Testament. Many people don't expect to find grace so powerfully expressed in the Old Testament. They think, *Old Testament: law and wrath. New Testament: faith and grace.* But no, the grace of God begins with the first book of the Bible and threads its way throughout the pages of the Old Testament until it finds its fulfillment in the revelation of Jesus Christ in the New Testament. The life of Joseph points to the life of Christ. The suffering of Joseph points to the suffering of Christ. The grace of Joseph points to the grace of Christ.

Joseph's words in Genesis 50:19 are so instructive for our own lives. He says to his brothers, "Don't be afraid. Am I in the place of God?" In other words, "You don't have to be afraid of me, because I'm not going to play God with you." For that's what revenge is really all about: playing God. When we set out to get even with someone else, we set ourselves up as the judge of that person's heart, conscience, and motives.

It's so tempting to play God, isn't it? It's tempting to inflict guilt and blame when someone has fallen and failed. It's tempting to play God when someone has confidentially shared with us a sin or struggle because now we can share that secret with others in order to ridicule or dishonor that person. It's so tempting to take vengeance into our own hands, even though Romans 12:19 tells us that vengeance belongs to God alone: "Do not take revenge, my friends, but leave room for God's wrath, for it is written: 'It is mine to avenge; I will repay,' says the Lord." When mistreated, we would do well to ask ourselves the question Joseph asked in Genesis 50:19: "Am I in the place of God?"

I remember sitting in my counseling room a few years ago with a couple whose marriage was disintegrating. The husband spoke first, listing all his grievances against his wife, including one particular sin she had committed almost ten years earlier. As he talked, his wife sat silently. When the husband had finished, there was a long, uncomfortable silence. Then, with a look of hurt in her eyes, she said, "You once told me you forgave me for that sin, but every time we argue, you bring it up again. If you've forgiven me, why won't you ever let me forget it?"

This marriage will never be whole until the husband is able to say, like Joseph, "Am I in the place of God?"

A little girl was once asked to define the word forgiveness. She thought a moment, then said, "I think it's like the pretty smell a flower makes when somebody steps on it." That's the kind of fragrance one catches from the life of Joseph: the fragrance of forgiveness and grace. Joseph had the power to put his brothers in chains. Instead, he liberated them. Joseph had the power to destroy his brothers. Instead, he built them up. Joseph had the power to inflict blame and guilt. Instead, he showered them with forgiveness and grace.

I know people who are contemporary Josephs—people who have gone through the most painful and bewildering trials of mistreatment. For a time, their faith was stretched to the limit, yet a few weeks, months, or years after their trial they came to me and said, "Ron, it's so clear now what God was doing. I can see how he has woven my hurt into a beautiful new pattern." They are living examples of the 50:20 Principle: "You meant it for evil, but God has used it for good."

One of the most successful and prolific authors in America was once a student at Ohio State University. There, his writing instructor told him, "Face it, young man. You don't have any talent for writing. My advice to you is to take a good, stiff dose of realism and go earn a normal living like everybody else."

The young writer's reply to the professor was angry and unprintable. He walked out of the class and never returned. A short time later, he went to New York City and began writing stories. During his first year as a full-time writer, he published over a hundred short stories. As they appeared in print, he sent a copy of each story to the Ohio State professor who had predicted his failure. Over the years, he sent this professor proof after proof that he had been wrong—photos of his awards, clippings of his reviews, and even a photocopy of his entry in *Who's Who*.

In a 1976 interview on NBC television, Tom Snyder asked him, "Are you a vengeful guy?"

His reply: "Oh, yeah, I think revenge is a good thing for everybody. . . . You've got to get even."

Now compare the perspective of this writer with that of radio talk show host Bruce Williams in a story he related to his NBC-radio "Talknet" audience, a story about his college days:

> I was a sophomore in my mid-twenties, married, two kids, making eighty dollars a week running the school snack bar. My boss was Professor So-and-so, who once ran a snack bar in a drive-in theater. One day I said, "Professor, it's pretty tough going through school and feeding a wife and two kids on eighty bucks a week. I need a raise."
>
> "Williams," he replied, "you have grandiose ideas. You'll never be worth a hundred dollars a week."
>
> Years later, I was invited to sit on the school's Board of Trustees. By this time, I

owned a few businesses, had been elected mayor of my community for a couple terms, and was hosting this thing I do on radio. I declined the invitation, but while I was on campus to meet the Board, I saw a door with Professor So-and-so's name on it. I raised my hand to knock—then I changed my mind and kept walking.

I had been prepared to go in and say, "Well, Professor, here I am with my grandiose ideas. I've got a feeling I make more in two weeks than you make in a year." But I thought, *What would that accomplish? Here I am, ready to pick on an elderly man who never really had much success in his life beyond getting out of the drive-in and getting his Ph.D.*

Then I realized I really owed him a debt, because whenever things got tough, I'd hear those words spurring me on, "Williams, you have grandiose ideas." In a perverse way, Professor So-and-so was my inspiration to succeed. Someday, I may go back and pay the professor a visit. But if I do, it'll be to thank him for telling me I had grandiose ideas.

What Bruce Williams discovered was a real-life application of the 50:20 Principle. Professor So-and-so meant his remarks for evil—an unfeeling and inconsiderate insult. But that insult was used for good in Williams's life, helping to inspire years of effort that have made him the most listened-to radio talk show host in America. That is the Joseph-like attitude that you and I must adopt in order to move beyond mistreatment—an attitude that rejects resentment and revenge, an attitude which says to our offender, "You meant it for evil, but God is going to use even this for his good in my life."

Notes

1. Frederick Buechner, *Wishful Thinking: A Theologlcal ABC* (New York: Harper & Row, 1973), p. 2.

CHAPTER FIVE

The Freedom of Forgiveness

History remembers Peter the Great, czar of Russia in the early eighteenth century, as one of the most beloved of all Russian rulers because of his wisdom, his compassion, and his efforts to modernize and reform his country. But there were people under Peter's rule who considered him too soft and benevolent. They wanted a czar with an iron fist, so they plotted Peter's death. The plot was discovered by the army. One of the conspirators, himself an army officer, was captured and thrown in a dungeon. There he was repeatedly tortured and interrogated, yet he refused to confess or reveal any details of the plot.

When Peter was told that one of the would-be assassins was being tortured in an army dungeon, he immediately went there. As Peter entered the dungeon, all the soldiers knelt in homage to their czar, yet Peter scarcely acknowledged their gesture. Instead he walked over to the poor wretch who hung in shackles against the wall. The man's flesh was bruised, slashed, and covered with burns from hot irons. Turning to the officer in charge of the torture, Peter said, "No amount of pain will make this man talk to you. But he will talk to me. Release him."

The prisoner lifted his head, a look of disbelief in his eyes, as his captors unshackled him. Too weak to stand, he sank to his knees. Tears streamed down the face of the czar as he bent toward the man and kissed him on the neck. "My friend, I know you plotted with other men to take my life, but you have suffered enough. Because of the mercy I show you, and because of the loyalty you owe me as your czar, I ask you to confess your crime. If you make an honest confession, I will not only forgive you, but will reinstate you as a colonel in the army." The man was so moved that he embraced Peter and made a full confession on the spot. True to his word, Peter reinstated the man with the rank of colonel.

That's the kind of forgiveness you and I are called to live out toward those who mistreat us. Forgiveness is therapeutic for the one who forgives—but more than that, forgiveness is a necessary precursor to reconciliation.

Charles Colson tells the story of a visit he made to the death row of the Indiana State Penitentiary.

Twenty Christian volunteers, led by Colson, were there to pray and share their Christian faith with the twenty condemned men in those cells. During the hour they spent there, two men in particular attracted Colson's attention. One was a black man, a convicted murderer whom I'll call Henry Lewis. The other was a white man, one of Colson's party of volunteers whom I'll call Tom Dodge.

Too soon, it was time to leave. Colson noticed Lewis and Dodge walking together in the corridor, heading slowly back to Lewis's cell. Colson caught up to them and said, "Tom, we have to go now. The warden's waiting to escort us out of the cell block."

Dodge turned, a look of grief on his face. "Chuck, I need just a few minutes more."

"I'm on a real tight schedule," Colson replied. "Some of us have other appointments."

"Please, Chuck," Dodge pleaded softly. "This is very important to me. You see, I'm Judge Thomas Dodge, and I'm the man who sentenced Henry Lewis to die. Since he came to this prison, Henry's become a Christian, my brother in Christ. We need just a few more moments to forgive each other and to pray for each other."

In that cell stood two very different men: one black, one white; one condemned, one the man who had pronounced the death sentence. Yet they stood with their arms around each other, expressing a kind of forgiveness and unconditional love that the world can't comprehend. If two men like Henry Lewis and Tom Dodge can be reconciled, then certainly reconciliation must be your goal and mine as we seek to move beyond our trials of mistreatment.

"God . . . reconciled us to himself through Christ," says 2 Corinthians 5:18, "and gave us the ministry of reconciliation." This is an important premise of the Christian life: You and I have been given the ministry, the task of reconciliation. Forgiveness and reconciliation is what our lives are to be about. Jesus came so that we could be reconciled to God and so that we might be reconciled to one another within the human family.

Yet, because of the brokenness of sin which infects us all, our relationships with each other too often are characterized by struggle, anger, and injustice. Reconciliation is hardly a simple matter. When one of our relationships has been marred by mistreatment, our goal must be to clarify communication and create understanding, to authentically and carefully listen to the other person's feelings and concerns. As we do so, we often see reconciliation take place.

Whenever two sides of a conflict are willing to commit themselves to the hard work of rebuilding trust and understanding, then a broken marriage, a damaged parent-child relationship, or a church division can be healed. In fact, the commitment and unconditional love of just one side of a conflict is often enough to melt the resistance of the other party and so bring about reconciliation.

But what about those times when the person with whom we wish to reconcile remains hardened and hostile? Or what if the mistreatment we experienced happened years or decades ago? What if the one who offended us is estranged from us, living in another state, or even dead? The offender is gone, but the bitter feelings remain. Can forgiveness take place without reconciliation?

Though reconciliation is always our goal, sometimes it is simply not possible. Over the years, I've counseled many people burdened with old memories and issues of mistreatment, people for whom reconciliation is impossible. There are even situations where reconciliation is, frankly, not desirable. Offenders who habitually mistreat others will frequently deny the wrong ever took place—often denying it even to themselves, blanking it out of their memories. Or they may verbally attack anyone who stirs up those memories. Attempting to reconcile with such a hardened individual may actually set back the healing process.

The good news, however, is that our emotional well-being does not depend upon what others do or fail to do toward us. Even when the offender chooses to leave the relationship broken, you and I can still be whole people. Forgiveness is unilateral, it is something we do all alone, right in our own hearts. Reconciliation depends on two people coming together, but forgiveness only depends on you.

When I'm counseling someone who has been through a trial of mistreatment, the question usually arises, "I'm willing to forgive, but the person who hurt me refuses to ask for forgiveness! How can I forgive someone who won't even admit he did anything wrong?" While I sympathize with this question, I have to state clearly that it does not reflect either a therapeutic or a biblical perspective on mistreatment. As long as the offender's actions remain pivotal to our willingness to forgive, we allow ourselves to be controlled by the offender.

When Jesus came into the world, he endured intense mistreatment. He was misunderstood, misjudged, falsely accused, beaten, whipped, tortured, and killed—and through it all, he never demonstrated any response other than forgiveness and unconditional love. He set the example for your attitude and mine. He exemplified the new perspective you and I must have on our trials of unfair treatment.

A major feature of this new Christlike perspective is this: When you and I are mistreated, our responsibility is to forgive and to release the past, no matter what the other person does. The offender's responsibility is just that: *his* responsibility. Our responsibility is to live free of resentment and bitterness.

Jesus said, "Love your enemies," and, "Bless those who curse you." Here again is a radical new perspective, a quantum leap beyond the old "eye-for-an-eye" attitude. And we wonder, "Why does Jesus place such a hard demand on us? If I'm supposed to 'love' people who are mistreating me—what's in it for me? Is Jesus suggesting that by 'loving' those who mistreat me, I may be able to win them over as friends?" I'm convinced the answer is no. Jesus was not giving us a prescription for manipulating our enemies into becoming our friends. Jesus knew that the enemy we bless will often continue to curse us.

But Jesus wasn't interested only in healing relationships. He was also interested in healing human hearts. If our offender continues in his sin, that's his problem. But if we continue to hate, that's a very real problem for us. A broken relationship is a tragedy but it's not the ultimate tragedy. The real tragedy is when we let someone else's hostility hold back our spiritual growth and emotional healing.

Forgiveness unlocks the past. It focuses our perspective forward, on the promise of the future, rather than backward, on old hurts. We mentally say to the person who offended us, "You did this to me, but I forgive you. Your mistreatment is no longer a factor in my life. Your actions can no longer affect my emotions." That is unilateral forgiveness. We may then approach the other person and seek bilateral, mutual forgiveness—that is, reconciliation. If the other person chooses to reconcile with us, then something beautiful takes place: a broken relationship is restored. But if that person persists in his hostility, reconciliation is a dead issue. Yet, though we can't always become friends with those who offend us, we can make the choice to become emotionally whole.

Matthew 18:21-22 describes the kind of radically new perspective we must discover in order to experience the freedom of forgiveness. Peter came to Jesus and asked, "Lord, how many times shall I forgive my brother when he sins against me? Up to seven times?" Peter wanted to know the boundary lines of forgiveness. He figured it would be quite generous to forgive someone seven times for a given offense. But Jesus' reply blew apart Peter's limited assumptions and confronted him with a new, limitless perspective: "I tell you, not seven times, but seventy times seven." In effect, Jesus was telling

Peter, "Forget about keeping track of each wrong you've forgiven, forget about limits, quit worrying about the boundary lines. Authentic forgiveness just keeps on forgiving."

You and I tend to be bound in our thinking by failed, shallow conceptions of forgiveness which say, "I'll forgive you—as soon as you apologize," or, "I'll forgive you—but I'll be watching every step you make," or, "I'll forgive you—as soon as I'm sure you've suffered enough," or, "I'll forgive you—just this once." But we will never know the true freedom of forgiveness until we adopt the radically new perspective Jesus taught and lived:

Forgiveness is unilateral.
Forgiveness doesn't depend on anyone
else's actions.
Forgiveness is final.
Forgiveness is complete.
Forgiveness erases blame.
Forgiveness is continual.

Jesus actively defined this kind of forgiveness as he hung dying on the cross. Even while his executioners were mocking, torturing, and murdering him, his prayer was, "Father, forgive them, for they do not know what they are doing" (Luke 23:34). Jesus did not wait for an apology, or for reconciliation, or for the punishment and repentance of his executioners. He simply and completely forgave.

Jesus' perspective on forgiveness is one which can carry us through every unfair trial we face in this life, even a trial which leads to death itself. One person who exemplified this Christlike perspective in the very moment of death was Edith Louisa Cavell, an English nurse who served with the Red Cross at the turn of the century. As director of the nursing staff at the Berkendael Medical Institute in Brussels, she helped to greatly improve the status and standards of nursing around the world. During World War I, when Belgium was overrun by the German army, she voluntarily remained at the Berkendael Institute and supervised its conversion into a Red Cross hospital. She also joined an underground movement which helped British, French, and Belgian soldiers escape to the Netherlands, a neutral country.

In August 1915, Edith Cavell was arrested by the Germans, along with a Belgian member of the underground, Philippe Baucq. By this time, she and Baucq had helped more than two hundred men escape to safety. Two months after their arrest, Cavell and Baucq were tried and sentenced to death. On October 11, they were led before a firing squad. As the German soldiers bound her to a post and blindfolded her, Edith turned to her condemned friend and said, "It is not enough to die for our countries. We must have no hatred or bitterness toward the Germans." Moments later, Edith Cavell and Philippe Baucq were dead.

Edith Cavell understood something about forgiveness that we, too, must understand. The goal of forgiveness is not just reconciliation. Nor is the goal of forgiveness just emotional healing. Ultimately, we forgive others because God has forgiven us. "Bear with each other," writes Paul in Colossians 3:13, "and forgive whatever grievances you may have against one another. Forgive as the Lord forgave you." The more completely we forgive, the more completely we identify with Christ. Our goal as Christians is to become more and more like Christ, and one way we do that is by forgiving like Christ.

During the writing of this book, I had several conversations with a close friend, Dr. James Osterhaus. Jim is a Christian psychologist and the author of *Counseling Families* (Zondervan, 1989). I am deeply indebted to him for many of the insights in this and other chapters of this book. In talking recently about forgiveness, he said to me, "Ron, one thing that people don't seem to understand when they hang on to their resentment is that by refusing to forgive, they are really denying the goodness of God. I've seen it again and again: The person who remains in bitterness eventually begins to direct that bitterness toward God. What that person is really saying is, 'All these experiences in my life added up to evil. How could God allow so much evil and mistreatment in my life?' The only healthy and realistic response is to realize that it's the painful things in life that God uses to build our character."

That's critically important for us to understand as we respond to our trials of unfair treatment. As Benjamin Franklin once said, "Those things that hurt us instruct us."

There's a scene in the motion picture *Ben Hur* that vividly illustrates what happens to anyone who rejects the freedom of forgiveness. The hero, Judah ben Hur, has suffered trial after trial of mistreatment, much like Joseph in the book of Genesis. Judah is Jewish, and his homeland, Israel, has been humiliated and enslaved by the Romans. Judah has spent years chained in the belly of a Roman slave galley. His mother and sister have contracted leprosy and live in a cave. A bitter hatred between Judah and a Roman named Messala—a hatred which culminates in the chariot race where Messala is killed—still stings Judah's heart.

Following the chariot race is a scene between Judah and Esther, the woman he loves. Judah seethes with bitterness. He vows to wipe out the Roman tyranny and cleanse the land with Roman blood. Esther, who just a few hours earlier sat at the feet of Jesus and listened to the Sermon on the Mount, replies, "The man I heard today on the hill said, 'Love your enemies. Do good to those who mistreat you.' " She then tells Judah she loves him and pleads with him to let go of his hate.

But Judah is hardened. Clutching the bitterness within him, he says, "You'd be better off if you didn't love me."

"It was Judah ben Hur I loved," she replies. "What has become of him? You've become the very thing you set out to destroy, giving evil for evil." Then she concludes with words that cut him to the heart: "It's as though you had become Messala!"

We each have a "Messala" in our lives— someone we resent, someone who has mistreated us. And if we don't summon the will to let go of those feelings, we will become the very thing we hate. It's as if our "Messala" actually enters into us, so that we become Messala, the offender. Ironically, that's the offender's greatest victory over us—the reshaping of our souls in his image.

That is why the cycle of mistreatment often replays itself over and over again. Somewhere in the distant past a father has mistreated a child. That child grows up bitter about his childhood. And upon whom does he take out his resentment? His own children. It goes on and on, generation after generation. Where will it stop? Each generation has to take responsibility for its own actions or the cycle will just keep repeating. Unless we consciously break the cycle of mistreatment, we will become the offender.

Over the years as I've counseled people in the aftermath of mistreatment, I've discovered a perspective on forgiveness that is often helpful: We may be better able to move beyond our mistreatment if we understand that our offender was in fact a broken person. When we see that there may have been factors in the offender's life that led him to be the way he is, our image of that offender changes. We experience an important perspective shift; we move from pure resentment toward that offender to understanding the offender.

Perspective is a key to forgiveness. A perspective which seeks to understand rather than hate parallels the perspective of Jesus on the cross. "Father, forgive them," he said, "for they do not know what they are doing." Jesus forgave his tormentors because he understood they didn't grasp the monstrous nature of their crime. That's a quantum leap in perspective.

When we experience that same quantum transformation in our perspective, then we can say, "Father, forgive that abusive stepparent, or that manipulative elder in my church, or that unfaithful spouse, or that rebellious child—because, Father, he just doesn't know what he's doing. I realize now he's had so much garbage in his own life that it's no wonder he treats people this way."

But let me underscore this: Understanding the offender's motivations doesn't mean we excuse sin. We are all responsible for our own choices. Yet, with such a shift in perspective, we can now view the offender in a different, more compassionate light. We now realize his attacks came from his inadequacy, insecurity, and hurt. This perspective shrinks the offender from a powerful, intimidating bully to something like a frustrated, powerless little boy.

Authentic forgiveness is nothing less than the power to liberate ourselves from the hurt of the past. When we make the choice to release the past with its bitterness and resentment, we regain control of our lives and our destinies. We become whole people once more.

There is a young widow living in Boston who has discovered a new perspective on mistreatment and forgiveness. Her name is Emily. She and her husband, a security guard, had only been married a few years when tragedy devastated her life. On April 11, 1983, Emily's husband walked across the parking lot of the shopping center where he worked. He was unarmed, escorting a merchant who carried two thousand dollars cash in a bag.

"Drop the bag!" said a voice behind them. The guard and the merchant turned and faced two men with shotguns. The manager dropped the money bag. One of the gunmen picked up the bag. The other opened fire. Emily's husband fell to the pavement with a massive hole in his upper body. Within minutes, he was dead. The gunmen got away.

The murder of her husband threw Emily into a tailspin of grief, anger, and depression. She tried to sublimate her bitter emotions by throwing herself into her job as a social worker, but she found that long hours of work only added exhaustion to her depression.

Time passed. One of the robbers, a tough young hood named Billy, was captured and brought to trial. Emily sat through the trial, churning with hatred. Even while justice was being done, she felt no sense of triumph—only a cold and disappointing bitterness. She realized that no jury verdict could ever repay her for the pain and loss of this crime.

The jury found the defendant guilty. When the judge asked Billy if he had anything to say before sentencing, something amazing happened: Billy stood and faced Emily. With tears in his eyes, he said, "I just wanted to say I'm really sorry." Then he sat down.

At that moment, something changed within Emily. In a sudden flash of understanding, she realized she would never be whole until she let go of the past. "I got tired of hating," she later told a reporter for the *Boston Globe*. "It takes an incredible amount of energy to hate, to be angry. I did that for five miserable years. My entire life was negative. . . .

"It took a lot for Billy to apologize. People will say he just did it to get a more lenient sentence. But I think it was too late for that. The judge had heard everything, and I think her mind was made up one way or the other. Besides, I don't care what other people think. I have to do what's right for me. Don't get me wrong. I do agree he needs to serve his time . . .

but I think he's changed, and I know I have. . . . Letting go of the anger was a big thing. Once I was able to let go and forgive, I could take control of my life."[1]

Emily discovered a quantum shift of perspective on her trial of mistreatment. Because she is living each day in the light of this new perspective, she now knows the freedom of forgiveness. As evidence of Emily's newfound focus on forgiveness rather than revenge, she has even promised to testify on Billy's behalf at his first parole hearing. Like Emily, you and I are discovering new perspectives on mistreatment. We are learning how to forgive. We are beginning to unlock the hurt of the past. And yet . . .

And yet many people experience a vague and disquieting feeling that forgiveness is not quite enough. Even when they decided to forgive, something holds them back from experiencing complete emotional healing. Within that mysterious and unknown depth of being called "the human heart," there is a throbbing pain, a remembrance of past hurts. If you identify with that feeling, you are not alone. I've often felt that way. Some of us need to take one more step beyond forgiveness. To be completely whole, we must also experience healing in our memories.

Notes

1. Kevin Cullen (Boston Globe reporter), "After 5 years, a widow stops hating," *San Francisco Examiner*, 18 December 1988, p. A-10.

CHAPTER SIX

The Healing of Memories

The tropical night air was filled with shouts and screams, mingled with the staccato of gunfire. Somewhere down the lane, a house burned. The scent of gunpowder was so heavy it settled on the tongue. When there is armed struggle in Central America, terror is everywhere.

Molly crept away from the window and hid herself behind a cabinet. Forty-two years old and alone, she had been a medical missionary in this land for many years and she deeply loved its lush beauty and gentle people. Now, for the first time since coming to this country, she was hiding in mortal fear.

She tensed as she heard footsteps outside the house. Then came a splintering crash as the door was kicked in. She clutched her mouth with both hands to keep from screaming. Heavy footsteps crossed the floor. Then she saw him. He was tall, muscular, and khaki-clad. A vicious-looking assault rifle loomed in her face. He called out, and soon a group of armed men crowded into the room.

Then began a trial more painful and humiliating than anything she could have imagined as, one by one, each man raped her in turn. Throughout her ordeal she cried out to God, begging him to make this terrible thing stop happening. But it went on for more than an hour. Finally the men went away. For a long time, all she could think was, *Why?! I've given you my life, everything I have to serve you in Central America! Why, God? Why did you let this happen?!*

Molly didn't expect an answer. But in those moments an answer came, almost as if Jesus himself were speaking in an audible voice: "Molly, I'm here with you. Remember, when you gave me your life, you gave me your heart. When you gave me your life, you gave me your mind. When you gave me your life, you gave me your body. Those evil men didn't do this just to you. They did it to me. There is no humiliation you can know that I have not known."

In the morning, when the village was safe for travel, Molly went to the mission hospital for treatment. Over the next few months, she confided in a couple of her closest friends about the assault, but never received professional counseling. As time passed, Molly was able to submerge her painful memories, though they continued to resurface in her nightmares.

In time, Molly returned to the United States on furlough. At home in upstate New York, she was speaking to a group of nursing students about her life as a medical missionary. As she spoke, she noticed a pair of girls in the audience, seemingly too young to be college students. During her talk, something kept drawing her glance toward those two girls. She felt an inner urging to depart from her notes, to let down her defenses, to share her most painful secret.

No! she told herself. *How can I share that horrible experience in a room full of strangers?!* But she knew it was God who was speaking to her.

She stopped in mid-sentence and looked around the room. All eyes looked back at her in puzzlement. Then, in a voice that quavered with emotion, she began to speak. She spoke tentatively at first—and then the story seemed to spill from her lips. Tears ran down her face and down the faces of many others in the room. When she had finished, she said, "I've never shared this story in public before, and I don't think I shall ever share it again. I don't know why, but I just felt God wanted me to say this today."

After most of the students had filed out, one of the two girls Molly had noticed came up to her. She seemed about sixteen years old. "Do you see my sister over there?" she said, pointing to the other girl, who remained in her chair. "Her name is Ann. She's fourteen. I think she's the reason God told you to tell that story. Ann was raped after school about two months ago. She won't talk to anyone anymore, not a word. She's been to our pastor and to psychologists and psychiatrists but she won't talk to them. Maybe she would talk to you."

Molly looked at Ann and their eyes met—then they ran to each other and embraced each other. They cried and they talked together for the next two hours. For the first time in weeks, Ann was talking, undamming a torrent of hurt and fear that she had clutched inside herself. For the first time since her assault, Ann had found someone who could identify with her pain. At the same time, Molly found a release from her inner brokenness by reaching out to help someone else. Together, Ann and Molly had taken a few tentative steps toward a place of healing—

The healing of memories.

For anyone who has endured the hurt of mistreatment, healing of memories is a crucial issue. Many of us desperately need to grow and change beyond our painful memories, to release the past and its pain, and to get on with our lives. Mentally, we know we should forgive and let go of old hurts—but at the level of our feelings, we are stuck in the past. We are angry. We feel violated and victimized. The hurt goes on hurting.

Again, the biblical story of Joseph points us toward workable, therapeutic solutions to the difficult problem of mistreatment. Remember that Joseph was a flesh-and-blood human being. Throughout his thirteen-year trial of mistreatment, he was kicked around by his family, by people he worked for, by people he trusted, by the society he lived in. He knew fear, anxiety, and depression, just as you and I do. Over the years, he stored up some painful, bitter memories. But, as we're about to see, Joseph was able to experience healing in his memories—and so can you and I.

Genesis 41 tells the story of Joseph's release from prison and his rise to a position of leadership and power in Egypt. In the course of his new career as prime minister of Egypt, he married an Egyptian woman named Asenath, who bore him two sons. In the context of this story are two verses—Genesis 41:51-52—which the casual reader might easily pass by. Yet these two verses mark a significant passage in the life of Joseph and carry a weight of meaning for your life and mine: "Joseph named his firstborn Manasseh and said, 'It is because God has made me forget all my trouble and all my father's household.' The second son he named Ephraim and said, 'It is because God has made me fruitful in the land of my suffering.' "

As was the custom in Old Testament times, Joseph gave his sons names with deeply significant meanings. The Hebrew of the name of his firstborn, Manasseh, can be translated "God has taken the sting out of my memories." The name of his secondborn, Ephraim, can be translated "God has made me fruitful." Joseph named these sons in remembrance of the great things God had done in his life.

I think I have a sense of how Joseph felt. My wife, Shirley, and I have two children, Rachael and Nathan. Rachael means "little lamb." Our "little lamb" weighed just two pounds when she was born eleven weeks prematurely, and for the first year of her life she suffered complications that required weeks in an incubator, later rehospitalization, and a full year of isolation at home. Today our Rachael is a healthy and happy teenager, and we are thankful for this "little lamb" and the joy she has given us.

Following her birth it appeared for a while that we would never have a another baby. A few years later, however, our second child was conceived. When this little boy was born safe and healthy, we named him Nathan, meaning "special gift." Sometimes when Shirley and I call our children by name, we do so as a remembrance of the meaning behind those names. So it was with Joseph. Two sons, Manasseh and Ephraim, two continual reminders of the goodness and graciousness of God.

May I make a suggestion? If you have been deeply mistreated, then in a spiritual sense you need to "give birth" to a Manasseh. You need to allow God to take the sting out of your memories. You need to experience the presence of God as he guides you through the corridors of your heart—corridors where pictures hang as painful reminders of the mother who berated you, of the father who neglected you, of the teacher who ridiculed you, of the spouse who was unfaithful, of the friend who betrayed you, of the employer who misjudged you, of the child who spurned your love. You need to look into the eyes of Jesus as he leads you through those musty corridors and as he takes down those ugly pictures and says, "These images can't hurt you any more. You're free."

Marjorie knows what I'm talking about. Her story was told to me by Kevin Ford. For years Marjorie had been burdened by broken self-esteem, seeing herself as unlovely, ungainly, untalented, unintelligent, un-everything that makes people feel valuable and worthwhile as human beings. Over the years, her self-hatred grew to a point where in desperation she turned to a Christian psychologist for help. He "walked" her back through her memories to a painful incident from her childhood.

Many years earlier, Marjorie had been caught in some minor act of misbehavior in her third-grade class. Her teacher—a harsh, vindictive discipli- narian—called Marjorie forward and stood her before the class. "Children," said the teacher, "I want each of you to come to the blackboard and write a sentence that begins with the word 'Marjorie.' Write anything you dislike about this bad girl."

The next few minutes were a waking nightmare for Marjorie as, one by one, each child went forward and chalked a hurtful statement about her in letters several inches tall. "Marjorie is ugly," wrote one. "Marjorie is fat," wrote another. "Marjorie is a slob." "Marjorie has no friends." "Marjorie is stupid." Standing before the class, Marjorie wished she could sink right through the floor and out of sight. It went on and on until all twenty-five classmates had filled the blackboard with hate and ugliness.

"Marjorie," said a kind voice.

Gradually, Marjorie realized she was no longer back in school. She was in the present, in the psychologist's office, and the kind voice she had heard was his. Tears flooded her face, and she was breathing deep, ragged sobs.

"Marjorie," the psychologist repeated, "I want you to picture the classroom again—but there's a difference this time. There's a twenty-sixth student in the classroom with you, and his name is Jesus. Now, imagine the scene with me: Jesus gets up from his desk and he walks past the teacher, ignoring the chalk she holds out to him. Instead of writing on the blackboard, he is erasing, erasing, erasing. Do you see it, Marjorie? The slate is clean now."

"Yes," she said. "Yes, I see it."

"Now Jesus takes up the chalk and begins to write. 'Marjorie is a beautiful child of God.' 'Marjorie is loved unconditionally.' 'Marjorie is forgiven.' 'Marjorie will live forever.' "

For the first time in many years, Marjorie began to feel valuable and loved. It was a giant first step along the path away from the crippling pain of mistreatment and toward wholeness.

Another woman I know, Joyce, desperately needs to give birth to a spiritual Manasseh. Thirty-eight years old and unmarried, Joyce lives in a large city on the West Coast. She has few friends, has difficulty relating to men on a social basis, and is often depressed. As a child, she was repeatedly abused, both physically and sexually, by her alcoholic father. Joyce's mother was aware of this abuse but did nothing to protect her. Joyce and her mother have never discussed these episodes and Joyce bitterly resents both parents. From the time she left home at sixteen, she has avoided contact with them.

Not long ago, she received a phone call from her mother. "Joyce, I just thought you ought to know—your father died this morning." Joyce said nothing, felt nothing. Her mother waited a few uncomfortable moments then said, "The funeral is going to be—"

"I'm sorry, Mother," Joyce interrupted, "but I can't come." Then she hung up. Anger boiled inside her. Suddenly, she felt all the old feelings again: terror and revulsion toward her father; the self-hate and guilt she took on herself because of her father's sin; the shame, violation, and betrayal. The man who had victimized her was now dead—yet the painful memories were still vividly alive.

Recently I described Joyce's story to my psychologist friend Dr. James Osterhaus and asked him what could be done to help her find emotional healing.

Jim described a helpful model aimed at leading Joyce to a place of healing and wholeness. I am indebted to him for most of what follows.

First of all, Jim said, Joyce needs to experience a shift in perspective on the mistreatment in her past. She must come to realize that by harboring bitterness toward her parents, she continues to let them victimize her. Joyce's mistreatment didn't end ten, twenty, or thirty years ago. It continues today because she maintains her parents in an important position in her life. Even though she walked away from her home long ago, she is still emotionally bound to her parents in a negative way. She needs to become emotionally free of her parents so they won't occupy such an important place in her present-day thoughts and actions.

A counselor might say to her, "Joyce, your parents abused you then, but you permit them to abuse you now. You allow those old events to continue replaying in your head and in your heart."

When Jim counsels someone who is hurting because of past mistreatment and there's no possibility of reconciliation, he often tries to help that person tell the offender "I forgive you" through a process called visualization.

It's important to note that visualization isn't something we choose to do or not do. In the sense Jim uses the term, it isn't something right or wrong. We all visualize, whether we know it or not. Visualization is natural and basic to who we are as human beings.

Some people have the mistaken idea that visualization is borrowed from Eastern religion. But the kind of visualization we have in mind here isn't at all like the New Age practice in which you "create your own reality," where you picture something in order to make it come true. Visualization is something we all do—we all use "mental pictures" to get our bearings or to give us a concrete handle on an abstract problem. We say that someone has a "stony heart" or that we're late and need to "run like the wind" or that our eccentric Aunt Gertrude's "elevator doesn't go all the way to the top." These are all pictures, mental handles . . . examples of visualizing.

Most of us don't control our visualization, even though it's possible to do so. We see inner images all the time, and some of this uncontrolled visualization generates anxiety in us. I might picture an ugly confrontation with a violent-tempered neighbor. Or I might lie awake wondering what my death will be like. I might picture myself speaking before a large audience, when suddenly my pants fall down. These forms of visualization cause anxiety. Why? Many psychologists believe that part of the brain doesn't distinguish between actual and imagined events.

When Jim helps a client visualize, he gives that client something more positive to dwell on so he or she will be less anxious. The person who says, "I get agitated when I remember how my father used to abuse me," must learn to show his or her brain another perspective on that event. Joyce, for example, might be able to say, "I see my father as a little boy. I realize he was abused as a child, and when he grew up he turned around and lashed out blindly at another child—and that child happened to be me. He couldn't stop himself. He was just an angry little boy who never grew up. Now I can forgive him."

David A. Seamands, the author of several important books on visualization and the healing of memories, says, "Healing of memories is a form of Christian counseling and prayer which focuses the healing power of the Spirit on certain types of emotional/spiritual problems. It is one and only one of such ministries; and it should never be made the one and only form."[1] I agree with him.

The ability to focus and meditate on positive thoughts is biblically wise advice. As Paul counsels in Philippians 4:8, "Whatever is true, whatever is noble, whatever is right, whatever is pure, whatever is lovely, whatever is admirable—if anything is excellent or praiseworthy—think about such things." When we change our thoughts, we are better able to change ourselves.

There are many biblical examples of visualization, especially the beautiful, soothing images David employs throughout the Psalms. Perhaps the most familiar images of all are found in Psalm 23:

The LORD is my shepherd, I shall not
    be in want.
He makes me lie down in green
    pastures,
he leads me beside quiet waters,
    he restores my soul.

It might be helpful for us to walk through a visualization experience. Let's say Joyce has come in to Jim for counseling. She's immobilized by resentment toward her father who just died. What would he say to her?

"I would begin with prayer," Jim told me, "asking God to guide us, because all healing comes from him. Then I might say to Joyce, 'I'm not going to end my prayer. I want you to keep your eyes closed. Joyce, I want you to go in your mind to a pleasant, relaxing place—the ocean, a mountain stream, your favorite quiet place. You see woods nearby, and you decide to take a walk there. Notice the sights and sounds around you. You're coming to a meadow, and as you approach it you see a hill on the far side of the meadow. There's a cross on that hill. You walk across the meadow and climb the hill. Now you see Jesus standing in the shadow of that cross—and there's someone else. It's your father, standing beside Jesus in the shadow of the cross. Now tell your father what God is telling you to say to him.'

"After she does this, I'd say, 'Now listen to what Jesus is saying to you.'"

This is a very emotional moment for many people. It creates an event, a memory in the person's mind—exactly like a good novel will do. It's as if she is actually with her father, experiencing this encounter in Christ's presence. She can still recall the old mistreatment as an event in history, but now she has a new event in her mind that is healing, refreshing, and reviving—an event infused with the presence of Christ.

Next, Jim might say, "Now, Joyce, take your father's hand and give it to Jesus. . . . Now say goodbye. . . . Now walk down the hill, back across the meadow, back into the woods, back into your place of quiet . . . back into this room."

That's one form of visualization, and it has been helpful for many who have trouble releasing resentment or grief. It's also helpful for those who have trouble forgiving themselves.

One woman came to Jim because of painful memories of an abortion she'd had as a teenager. He walked her through this process and had her give her baby to Jesus.

"It was the most powerful counseling situation I've ever been in," Jim said. "At the end she said, 'Now I know Jesus has my baby and everything's okay.' It was so touching. She had us both crying by the time it was over! And she's never had to worry about the baby since."

How does the healing of memories work, and why do we sometimes need to take a step beyond forgiveness in order to find emotional healing?

The problem is that forgiveness is essentially a decision, rooted in the will and the intellect. And while you and I may intellectually accept the fact that we should release the past and get on with our lives, emotionally we just can't do it. Somehow, we have to find a way to pull our feelings in line with what our mind knows we should do.

Many psychologists believe that we are two-brained people, with a left and right brain. According to this theory, the two halves of our brain are almost like two independent brains, each with its own way of thinking, connected by a slender bridge called the *corpus callosum*. The logical, analytical left brain is the side mostly responsible for language. It processes data in a computer-like fashion, point by point, and arrives at rational decisions. The right brain, however, is intuitive, not detail-oriented. It does not analyze. It has no speech centers. The right brain understands metaphor, receives artistic impressions, and appreciates poetry. It's also the side that experiences and remembers feelings.

A lot of people have no trouble forgiving in the intellectual, logical, linear left brain. But on the right side of the brain—the subjective, impulsive, rela-tional side—our feelings are still chained down. Intellectually I may say, "I forgive you," but there's a part of me that still remembers the mistreatment. That's where healing of memories comes in. This kind of healing is not an intellectual, left brain exercise at all. If it were, all a counselor would have to do is explain forgiveness and we'd be cured.

Healing of memories has to take place at the experiential and feelings level. It has to reorder our perspective and change our feelings associated with the mistreatment. We don't need to have our intellects walked through a visualization process. It is our emotions which need to experience a memorable event fragrant with the healing presence of Christ.

The Bible often speaks about the difference between the "head" and the "heart." In today's clinical terms, we might express it as the difference between the left and right brain. Jesus said, "Why do you call me 'Lord, Lord' [left brain intellectual knowledge], and do not do what I say?" [right brain action and experience from an internalized belief]. Faith that is not acted upon accomplishes nothing.

Clearly, the logical, left brain side is important to the overall healing process. We must be transformed not only in our feelings, but in our perceptions, our actions, and our will. Both right and left brain change must take place. The "head" must assent to the truth that forgiveness is the way to live and that bitterness is destructive. When this "head" knowledge becomes a "heart" experience, we will be emotionally healed.

Convincing the left brain is the easy part of the healing process. Right brain healing is a more elusive proposition. Let's use a young man called "Joe" as an example of why purely left brain approaches to forgiveness fail.

Suppose Joe attends a seminar and comes away with a set of principles, "Six Steps to Forgiveness," which he duly impresses upon his left brain. Then he goes to Dick, a friend with whom he has had a minor conflict. Having memorized the "Six Steps" word for word, he woodenly recites, "Step One: Dick, I have something against you." Joe proceeds to go through all six steps by the numbers, yet inside he is still boiling with anger toward Dick. What's worse, Dick becomes angry because he senses Joe's hostility and thinks, *Hey, this guy's still attacking me!*

This relationship cannot be healed without a right brain transformation within Joe—a change marked by a sense of brokenness and humility on Joe's part, along with a recognition of his own sin and flaws.

I've been applying these principles and lessons to my own broken memories. I'm still on a journey of discovery, still finding new perspectives, still mending. But these insights have already proved practical, workable, and therapeutic in my own life, and I'm thankful to Jim for helping me move a few important steps closer to wholeness. I trust these insights will prove valuable in your journey as well.

Clara Barton, the founder of the American Red Cross, had a well-known reputation as someone who never held a grudge. Once, when a friend reminded her of a wrong done to her some years earlier, she seemed not to know what her friend was talking about. "Surely you must remember!" said the friend.

"No," Clara replied without hesitation. "I distinctly remember forgetting that."

Like Clara Barton, you and I can experience healing in our memories. Even though we may never be able to forget the mistreatment that occurred in our past, we can be healed of its pain. We can experience the meaning of "Manasseh," and we can say with Joseph, "God has taken the sting out of my memories."

Notes

1. David A. Seamands, *Healing of Memories* (Wheaton, Illinois: Victor Books, 1985), p. 24.

CHAPTER SEVEN

Courage to Confront

Linda, a mother of three small children, knew her marriage was crumbling. Her husband was spending his off-hours with the office bookkeeper. Linda suspected adultery, but instead of directly confronting her husband she nagged him about spending so much time away from home. Eventually, Linda's husband admitted the affair, but Linda was so afraid of losing him that instead of confronting him, she agreed to allow him to bring his lover into their bedroom. Linda's confusion and hurt deepened as the affair was carried out right in front of her. Yet, out of a desire to be "loving" (and with a tragic misunderstanding of what that word means), Linda put the "needs" of her husband and his illicit lover above her own needs. She failed to confront.

This story of mistreatment and looming tragedy is detailed in James Dobson's book *Love Must Be Tough*. Dr. Dobson warned that if Linda would not take immediate steps to confront her husband's sin head-on, her "tolerance and longsuffering will probably be fatal to her marriage."[1] Clearly, Linda's trial of mistreatment is extreme in its scope and its urgency, and she will need the guidance of a professional counselor to find the best way to confront her husband's mistreatment.

The pain in your relationship may be of a different degree and kind, but one lesson from Linda's story clearly applies to you and me: Sometimes love must be tough, sometimes love must confront. As 1 Corinthians 13:6 tells us, "Love does not delight in evil but rejoices with the truth." It is not always genuinely loving to be "tolerant" and "longsuffering" when someone mistreats us. It may simply be that we wish to avoid the unpleasant emotions of confrontation. Or we may lack assertiveness. Or we may be afraid. The result of such timidity or indifference can lead to tragedy.

Dr. Hyder was the pastor of a large church on the East Coast. The people of his church loved him for his warm and caring manner and his genuine compassion for others. Because of their affection for him, the people in Dr. Hyder's church were willing to overlook his one major flaw: Dr. Hyder had a drinking problem.

At first, only a few people in the church office knew about it, then the church board became aware of it, and finally word of Dr. Hyder's problem spread through the congregation. People talked about it among themselves, but nobody talked to Dr. Hyder. "He's such a wonderful man," they said, "and after all, nobody's perfect. We can afford to be tolerant of one or two faults in such a caring and capable pastor." But Dr. Hyder's drinking problem continued to grow until it interfered with his preaching, his counseling, and his administration of church business. Even so, no one talked to him about it.

One morning, the church secretary opened the door to Dr. Hyder's office and found him on the floor behind his desk, dead. He had taken his own life. On the desk was a note in Dr. Hyder's handwriting, consisting of just one line: "Why didn't any of you care enough to help me?" A life was destroyed because an entire church was afraid to speak the truth in love.

It's in the apostle Paul's famous "Love Chapter" of 1 Corinthians 13 that verse 6 says, "Love does not delight in evil but rejoices with the truth." If we say we love someone, how can we allow him or her to continue in destructive behavior? If we are afraid to speak the truth, how can we claim to genuinely love? If we blithely allow someone to continue in behavior that is destructive, abusive, unethical, or immoral, then we are not acting in love. We are actually enabling and contributing to the brokenness of that person. Such behavior—which we try to pass off as "tolerance"—is worse than hatred. For it is really indifference, the true opposite of love.

It's so easy to fool ourselves by thinking, *I really shouldn't confront him. I should be tolerant and loving*. But are we being "loving" when we shrink from confrontation? Or are we just being cowards? Look at it another way. Suppose we see one of our children run out onto a busy freeway and we fail to confront that behavior, thinking, *I don't want to mess up his day. He's having so much fun out there on the freeway.* The absurdity of such an example is plain. If we love that child, we'll run out and pull him to safety. If we authentically love someone who is engaged in a lifestyle of sin, we will confront that destructive behavior.

Some people think the response God wants from us is to stay in an abusive situation and bear it. But is that really what God wants? The story of a young woman named Ellen may help bring this question into sharper focus.

Ellen is an attractive woman in her early thirties, living in a large city in the South. Several years after her marriage to Brian, a salesman for a major manufacturing corporation, Ellen made a decision to give her life to Jesus Christ. Her husband, however, wanted nothing to do with her newfound faith.

Brian was a major sales producer for his company—a successful, ambitious, driven man. As a result, he fell into a fast-track lifestyle of high spending, hard drinking, and cocaine. He refused to let his wife attend church, tried to get her to join him in his drug abuse, and several times beat her while he was drunk. Fearing for her life, Ellen phoned her friend Susan for advice. Because Brian had cut her off from her church and her Christian friends, it had been months since she had talked to Susan. After pouring out her story, she concluded, "Susan, I'm just so scared all the time. I don't know what crazy thing he's going to do next! I want to leave him, but I don't know where to go, unless—unless you would let me stay at your house."

"Absolutely not!" said Susan. "Don't you know the Bible says a wife must submit to her husband no matter what he does? Ellen, I know things must be terribly hard for you right now, but I'm afraid all I can do for you is pray that Brian will change."

But the only change Ellen saw in her husband was a change for the worse. A few days after her talk with Susan, Brian came home and told her about a big deal he was on the verge of closing. There was just one thing he wanted Ellen to do that would clinch the sale: He wanted her to go to bed with his client. When she refused, Brian slapped her. "Don't argue with me!" he roared. "Just do it!" He handed her a slip of paper with the hotel and room number where the man was waiting. Then he called a taxi to pick her up.

Brian walked Ellen to the curb and saw her step meekly into the cab. He handed the driver two twenty-dollar bills, gave him the address, and waved them off. As the cab pulled away, Ellen's cheeks were burning and her stomach was knotted. It was a twenty-minute drive downtown. When the cab was within a few blocks of the hotel, Ellen shouted, "Driver, stop right here!"

"But, lady, your husband said—"

"Now!"

The cab rumbled to a halt. Ellen threw open the door and ran to a pay phone at the corner. Rummaging in her purse, she found two quarters. She put one in the phone and called Susan. Breathlessly, she told Susan what Brian had ordered her to do. "Susan, what do I do now?"

There was a long pause, then Susan said, "Ellen, the Bible says a wife is to submit to her husband—"

Suddenly furious, Ellen shot back, "Doesn't the Bible also say, 'Thou shalt not commit adultery'?" Then she slammed the phone down. She had one more quarter. "Please let him be there—" she prayed quickly as the coin dropped into the machine. She dialed, then waited.

"Hello?" said a voice in the receiver.

"Hello, Pastor Hartwell. I don't know if you remember me after all these months, but my name is Ellen Rowe—"

"Of course I remember you, Ellen. How are you?" For a few seconds, she was unable to speak. Then she began to cry in hard, choking sobs. "I'm desperate," she finally said. And she poured out her story to Pastor Hartwell.

"Is the cab still waiting for you?" he asked when she had finished. She glanced at the street. The driver had pulled the cab to the curb and was pacing the sidewalk. "Yes," she said.

"Good. Get back in that cab and have the driver bring you to my house. My wife and I will put you up until you can get things settled with your husband."

Over the next few days, Ellen tried to get her husband to go into marriage counseling with her. He not only refused, but threatened her. He was enraged over the lost deal because she hadn't shown up at the hotel. Though she tried for several months to reconcile with him, he was completely intransigent. Eventually, he filed for divorce.

Today, Ellen's marriage is broken, but she herself is whole—physically, spiritually, and emotionally whole. She learned, just in time, that there is a greater kind of submission that God expects than the submission of a wife to her husband: obedient submission to God.

When one person in a marriage is involved in immorality, unethical behavior, intimidation, manipulation, or abuse, the other partner has an obligation to challenge that behavior—even to the point of creating a crisis in the marriage. This is what Ellen did when she refused to go to that hotel room and instead sought Christian counsel and shelter from Pastor Hartwell.

If you fail to confront the behavior of the person who is abusing you, you clearly do yourself no favor—but you also are doing the abuser a disservice. By continuing in the role of the ever-tolerant, subservient victim, you actually endorse and enable the abuser's behavior. That's not submission as the Bible describes it; that's just slavery. Authentic love does not delight in evil but rejoices with the truth.

The Bible clearly teaches that submission is a two-way street. A close examination of Ephesians 5 reveals that wives are to submit to their husbands, husbands are to sacrificially love their wives as Christ loved the church, and at all times, in all ways,

Christians are to submit to each other for the building up of God's church. "Submit to one another," says Ephesians 5:21, "out of reverence for Christ."

I feel strongly about this issue because I've seen the fallout from the false view that a "submissive" wife should be a doormat for an abusive husband. I've seen women with physical scars inflicted by abusive husbands—scars that go much deeper than the flesh, scars that reach to the depths of the soul. It is not an act of love for a woman to submit to such mistreatment. Love demands that the abuser be confronted. (And so, by the way, does the law. Abusers are lawbreakers and should not be shielded from the consequences of their criminal behavior.)

As in every issue surrounding the problem of mistreatment, the key to healing is perspective. "When I counsel someone who is undergoing extreme and ongoing mistreatment," said my friend Jim Osterhaus, "I always try to change that person's perspective. I confront the idea that this person should simply accept mistreatment. If a woman objects and replies, 'But the Bible says to turn the other cheek,' I answer, 'Do you think permitting your husband to humiliate and beat you is the best witness to him as to what a man should do with a woman? Does it honor God to allow him to continually abuse you? And is this the best statement to you about what a woman is in God's eyes? Didn't God create women to be more than meek little punching bags for men?' "

I think secular approaches go at it the wrong way. They say, "Look, you're a person with rights and nobody has the right to dump on you." But as a

Christian, I don't think the issue is "rights." The issue is God's image. When you allow yourself to be abused, you cheapen the image of God in your spouse and in yourself. You permit the abuser to mar his own image and to mar your own image.

"Whenever physical abuse takes place," Jim told me, "I urge the person to get out of the situation immediately. Not long ago, I was talking to a woman whose husband had seriously beaten her several times. She said, 'You know, I still can't be around my husband without feeling nervous.' 'Congratulations!' I replied. 'That's the way you should feel! You're responding the way God designed you to, because you're in danger.' "

In a moment of rage, a physically abusive person is capable of anything. Spouses of abusers have been maimed, disfigured, paralyzed, and killed. Physical abuse is something you don't take chances with.

I always try to move a person out of the victim role and sometimes that means mistreatment must be challenged. The offender must be confronted with his sin. It's not God's ideal for us to allow others to abuse us. Yes, God wants us to bear mistreatment without hatred and bitterness. But he also wants us to be witnesses to his own image which is stamped upon us. That means that to love, we must sometimes challenge sin. We must say, "Stop!"

Occasionally there are extreme situations in which people are mistreated and there's nothing they can do about it—for example, when someone is being held hostage by terrorists or is suffering for his faith in a Communist prison. But even when a person is helpless to change the external circumstances, he or she can still choose the right perspective. That person can still choose to respond without bitterness or resentment.

Loving confrontation is not an easy thing to do. Some people avoid confrontation at all costs; they either give in or withdraw from an uncomfortable situation. Others see confrontation as the opportunity to ventilate their anger and perhaps even get revenge. Their goal is not to solve the problem but to win the fight. Neither of these extremes is biblical or therapeutic.

God calls us to a more creative approach to conflict, an approach that does not give up, run away, or strive to dominate. God's creative solution to conflict is *resolution*. By his grace we seek to resolve our conflicts and come together in love. Even though reconciliation is not always possible because of the hardened attitude of the other person, reconciliation is always our goal, and love—not bitterness or revenge—must always be our motive.

A trial of mistreatment is an opportunity to take stock of our commitment to unconditionally love those who hurt us. We know Jesus commanded us to love our enemies, but what does that mean? Often it means we must love the offender enough to go to him or her in private and say, "I feel hurt by what you did. What's more, I think you've hurt yourself by what you did. I love you and believe in you enough to take the risk of telling you how I feel. I want to pray with you about this. I want to be your friend."

This is what Jesus means when he says in Matthew 18:15, "If your brother sins against you, go and show him his fault, just between the two of you.

If he listens to you, you have won your brother over." And the apostle Paul describes the godly attitude for loving confrontation in Galatians 6:1—"Brothers, if someone is caught in a sin, you who are spiritual should restore him *gently.* But watch yourself, or *you also may be tempted*" (emphasis added). Loving confrontation is always gentle and humble. Its goal is always to heal, never to back the offender into a corner or extract an apology. To restore a broken relationship, we must build the other person up, not tear him down.

Before confronting, we look first to our own hearts: Are we confronting out of genuine love for the offender or because we can't wait to set him or her straight? Do we choose words that heal or words that hammer home our point? Do we approach the offender in loving sorrow over the broken relationship or do we attack him in anger? Do we genuinely want to rebuild the relationship or do we just want to get something off our chests?

When we've done all we can to purify our motives, then it's time to act. Children may run from confrontation, but adults must stay and meet it head-on. Maturity demands that we courageously, lovingly face those who mistreat us with a goal of bringing about resolution and reconciliation.

In her book *Loving Confrontation*, Beverly Caruso says that before approaching anyone about a hurt or disagreement, she sits down and reads through 1 Corinthians 13 while mentally picturing the person she feels called to confront. This helps her to see that offender in the light of God's love, which in turn enables her to feel love for that person. Then she is able to go to that person with an attitude of affirmation. She goes on to explain what she means by affirmation:

> Some of us who don't like confrontation at all (and I fall into this category) have a tendency to try to smooth conflict over before we've gotten to the root of it. Affirmation doesn't mean starting off with a list of compliments. Maybe you've had a friend launch into a long catalog of your "good points," with the uncomfortable sense that you know what's coming. You're being fattened for the kill. This approach actually makes you feel wary and ready to defend yourself.
>
> Rather, you should begin by underscoring these two things: your commitment to the individual and to the relationship; your eagerness to listen to their viewpoint. This will affirm your friend's value at a much deeper level than a listing of favors they've done or characteristics that you like about them.
>
> Then, I simply go ahead and explain the way I view the circumstances about which I'm bothered. At this point, it's wise to stick to the facts, reconstructing the events and what was said as clearly as you can recall. Along with listing the outward circumstances, it's also fair to state how the circumstances made you feel. Never attack ("You did that just to hurt me"). Never judge and label ("You're the biggest gossip

I know"). Simply state your inner response ("It hurt me. In fact, I got angry").[2]

When you feel called to confront someone, keep these points in mind:

1. Go in an attitude of prayer. Seek God's wisdom and guidance.

2. Be gentle and humble. Be aware of your own feelings and motives. Be aware that you, too, may be the offender some day. How would you want someone to confront you about your behavior?

3. Be prepared to listen and learn. Be willing to be influenced by the other person's facts and perceptions.

4. Affirm your commitment to the other person and to the relationship.

5. Be patient. Stay calm. Expect the other person to be defensive.

6. Never attack. Never judge the other person's inner motives.

7. Be specific. Don't generalize. Say, "I was hurt by that remark you made about me in front of our guests last night," not, "You're always abusive and insulting."

8. Recognize that it takes a lot longer to heal a relationship than to hurt it. If your dialogue reaches a point of impasse, be sensitive to the fact that you may need to withdraw from each other for a time and re-attempt the reconciliation process sometime later.

9. If you get nowhere one-on-one, be ready with a suggestion that a third person might be able to help the two of you shape the conversation in a more constructive way. Choose someone you both consider mature, wise, and neutral.

10. End your dialogue with prayer. Reemphasize your commitment to be a friend to the other person.

Many passages in the Bible talk about loving confrontation. One such passage that is especially meaningful to me is from Proverbs 27:6—"Faithful are the wounds of a friend" (NASB). I can personally testify to the truth of those words. One Sunday morning, back in the days when I was fresh out of graduate school and serving in a large church in the Midwest, I was speaking on the subject of compassion for the needy and spiritually lost in the world. This was in the 1970s, when Hal Lindsey's *The Late Great Planet Earth* was a runaway bestseller and Bible prophecy had taken its place on the social scene alongside such fad-fascinations as UFOs, astrology, the occult, and great white sharks.

In the course of my talk, I made the statement, "Some of us in this church would do well to be as concerned about reaching the poor and the lost for Christ as we are about every little detail of Bible prophecy."

Immediately after the church service, a close friend of mine, an older man named Ed, gently took me aside and said, "Ron, I really appreciated your message this morning. But there was one statement you made that I think was probably more hurtful than helpful to our church. It was the statement about Bible prophecy versus caring about the poor and the lost. You see, there's a very godly man in our congregation, Mr. Lake, and he works very hard each week teaching an adult Sunday school class on Bible prophecy. He puts in many hours studying Daniel, Revelation, and other passages of the Bible and trying to apply these passages to the world we're living in today. I have a feeling your comments this morning probably hurt Mr. Lake."

In a very gentle and caring way, my friend Ed had confronted me. I know it couldn't have been an easy thing for Ed to do, but he courageously did so because he cared for Mr. Lake—and because he cared for me. I knew Ed was right, so I got together with Mr. Lake and talked to him about my comments. He acknowledged he had been hurt by what I said. I asked his forgiveness, and as we prayed and reconciled with each other, I discovered a new depth of friendship and respect for Mr. Lake. Whenever I hear those words from Proverbs, "Faithful are the wounds of a friend," I think of my friend Ed, who loved me enough to confront me when I was wrong.

I need to have people in my life who are courageous and caring enough to confront me. So do you. Moreover, you and I need to become the kind of people who will care—and dare—to lovingly confront those who mistreat us. As Ephesians 4:15 tells us, " . . . speaking the truth in love, we will in all things grow up into him who is the Head, that is, Christ." As we learn to face mistreatment boldly, unflinchingly, yet without bitterness or resentment, we move closer and closer to our ultimate goal as Christians: having the mind, character, and attitude of Jesus Christ.

Notes

1. Dr. James C. Dobson, *Love Must Be Tough* (Waco, Texas: Word Books, 1983), p. 16.

2. Beverly Caruso, *Loving Confrontation* (Minneapolis: Bethany House Publishers, 1988), pp. 28-29.

CHAPTER EIGHT

The Power of
Positive People

Thomas Edison, the holder of 1,093 patents on inventions ranging from the electric light bulb to the phonograph to the motion picture projector, was an optimist extraordinaire. When he was sixty-seven years old, a fire swept the buildings of his laboratory, destroying prototypes, plans, notes, sketches—the work of many years. The fire burned fiercely through the night and was only barely controlled by sunrise. That morning, as smoke continued to rise over the work of a lifetime, Edison called his employees together in the grounds by the ruined buildings. The same questions ran through everyone's minds: Is Edison ruined? Will his spirit be broken? How can a sixty-seven-year-old man start over from nothing?

Edison climbed onto a salvaged lab table and said, "You people are probably thinking, *Well, the old man is licked for sure.* Hogwash! Today's just an ordinary workday, and everyone still has his job to do. Only difference is, instead of working in our laboratory, we'll be rebuilding it."

Immediately he began assigning tasks to his employees. One man was detailed to locate new lab equipment. Another was sent to the railroad office to arrange shipping. Another was sent to hire a contractor to oversee reconstruction. Then, almost as an afterthought, Edison added, "By the way, does anybody know where we can get some money?"

Edison's son was standing nearby, amazed at what he was hearing. When all the employees had gone to carry out Edison's orders, the young man said, "Dad, how are you going to rebuild after a disaster like this? You don't have any capital."

Edison clapped a hand on his son's shoulder and said, "Son, you can always make capital out of disaster. We'll build bigger and better out of these ruins." And with that, Edison rolled up his coat, set it on the table for a pillow, crawled onto the table, and went to sleep.

There is an incredible power in positive people like Edison—power to move on in the face of discouragement, power to take disaster and reshape it into achievement. What an example this man set for his son and for the people who worked under him! I want to be that kind of man. I want my life to express that kind of power—the power of positive people.

Edison was unstoppable because he was one of the world's greatest optimists. At age forty, Edison had reaped an astounding four million dollars in royalties from his invention of the electric light bulb. He then spent five years, from 1887 to 1892, trying to develop a magnetic process for separating iron from low-grade ore. Finally, he gave up—but not until he had spent his entire four million dollar fortune. "Well, it's all gone, the whole four million!" he told his associates with characteristic good cheer. "But didn't we have a good time spending it!"

Edison was unstoppable because he didn't let past disappointments shape his future. He once performed fifty thousand experiments in an attempt to invent a long-life electrical storage battery. Though none of those fifty thousand approaches worked, Edison refused to label his project a failure. When someone asked how he could persist in experiment after experiment without results, Edison replied, "Results? Why, I've gotten plenty of results! I now know fifty thousand things that won't work!" (Incidentally, he finally built and patented that battery.)

Edison was unstoppable because he never gave up on the future. He never stopped working, never stopped risking, never stopped being fascinated by the things around him. Once, when asked to sign a guest book, he wrote his name and address in the appropriate columns and in the last column, which was headed "Interested in," he wrote, "Everything." He continued to be fascinated by everything around him throughout his life. Just before his death at age eighty-four, Edison was working on a formula for synthetic rubber.

In his book *There's a Lot More to Health Than Not Being Sick*, Bruce Larson tells the story of his youngest son Mark who, at the age of twenty, bought his first ten-speed bicycle. The day after he purchased his new bike, a major bike race was scheduled to take place in nearby Fort Myers, Florida. Many of the most experienced bicycle racers in the state were scheduled to compete. Mark, without any training or experience, with only his shiny new one-day-old bike, signed up for the race. Bruce tried to dissuade his son, telling him that the top racers spent many years training and learning how to race competitively. Mark just shrugged. "It'll be a good experience," he said.

At the end of the race, Mark was handed the first-place trophy. Bruce was dumbfounded. "How did you 'do it, Mark?" he stammered. "I mean, how did you beat all those experienced racers?"

"Well, Dad," Mark said, waxing philosophical, "long distance bike racing is pretty tricky. To race professionally, you have to know how to pace yourself and just when to make your move. Well, I don't know any of that stuff, so I just took off and pedaled as fast as I could. Fortunately, nobody ever passed me."

"The moral is obvious," Larson concludes. "No one is too inexperienced. No one is too young or too old. We can all have an exciting future. When we cease to be excited about our futures, we have lost touch with God. Find Him again, and hope will spring in our hearts. We can tap into the dreams and visions He has for us."[1]

Turning again to the story of Joseph, we see a young man who endured mistreatment with an attitude of godly optimism. Joseph always looked forward with hope and backward with forgiveness. He had learned, through trial after trial of mistreatment, to always say yes to life. Throughout his story, we see evidence upon evidence of the power of a positive person.

He endured thirteen years of "bad luck"— rejection by his brothers, slavery, slander, imprisonment, abandonment. He persevered through those long and disappointing years. He built character, acquired wisdom, and tempered his faith. And when he emerged from prison and was elevated to prime minister over Egypt, this positive, visionary young man engineered a massive food reserve program that saved Egypt and the surrounding region from starvation. Joseph had confidence that, with God working through him, he could accomplish anything.

Yet the story of Joseph, in the closing chapters of Genesis, is a story of remarkable contrasts. For while Joseph is achieving great things in Egypt, his father Jacob is on the family farm up north in Canaan. Unlike his long-lost son Joseph, Jacob is gloomy, sullen, depressed, immobilized. These two men, Joseph and his father Jacob, remind me of the lines by Frederick Langbridge in *A Cluster of Quiet Thoughts*: "Two men look out through prison bars: One sees the mud, and one the stars."

Joseph knows what it's like to look out from prison bars but he doesn't know what it means to be defeated by them. In his prison time, Joseph was a stargazer. He had faith in God and belief in himself. He looked up and saw the stars.

Jacob, on the other hand, was too often a mudgazer, inhabiting the prison of his own bitter emotions. Unlike Joseph, unlike Edison, unlike Bruce Larson's hard-pedaling son, Jacob held out no hope for the future. He was a negative force in his family. In his earlier days, he conspicuously favored Joseph while treating the rest of his sons like hired hands. In his later life, he transferred his favoritism from his lost son to Joseph's little brother Benjamin—while continuing to berate and belittle his other sons, breaking their self-esteem and incurring their resentment.

Certainly the world Jacob faces in Genesis 42 and 43 is hard and troubled. Famine is everywhere. Jacob believes his son Joseph is dead. He sends his sons to buy grain from Egypt, unaware that the Egyptian prime minister in charge of food reserves is his own lost son Joseph. But when they return, they are short one son: the Egyptian prime minister (Joseph) was holding Jacob's son Simeon hostage to force the brothers to return with Benjamin. "You have deprived me of my children," Jacob accused his sons in Genesis 42:36. "Joseph is no more and Simeon is no more, and now you want to take Benjamin. Everything is against me!"

Jacob's words drip with self-pity and blame. "Everything is against *me*!" he complains. He is immobilized by bitterness. He knew the "Egyptian" had ordered him to send his sons back with Benjamin or there would be no more grain. Yet he does nothing while the family larder grows emptier and emptier. Finally, as his family scrapes the bottom of the barrel in Genesis 43:1, Jacob says to his sons, "Go back and buy us a little more food."

Jacob's sons are incredulous. Had their father lost his mind? Didn't he remember that they had been told not to return for more food without their little brother Benjamin? When they remind him of this fact, Jacob explodes in anger, "Why did you bring this trouble on me?" Again: blame, accusation, self-pity.

There's an old adage that an optimist sees an opportunity in every calamity, while a pessimist sees a calamity in every opportunity. What is your perspective on your trial of mistreatment? Does it look like a calamity or an opportunity? Your answer to that question will have a profound effect on your ability to reshape your future and move beyond mistreatment.

As I've been examining Joseph's story during the writing of this book, one fact that keeps leaping out at me is that there is more space given to Joseph than to Adam, Noah, Abraham, Isaac, Jacob, or any other character in Genesis. And we have to pause and wonder: Why does God in his Word spend so much time on the life of Joseph? I have to conclude that it's not because Joseph was some sort of super-saint, or because of his keen intellect, or because of his leadership skills. Rather, I believe the one unique quality that distinguished Joseph was his attitude.

Joseph was a flesh-and-blood human being, no different from you and me. The one truly supernatural dimension to this man was the positive, forgiving way he faced life. Elbert Hubbard once wrote, "The final proof of greatness lies in being able to endure contemptuous treatment without resentment"—and by this definition, Joseph was indeed a man of greatness.

I believe the secret of Joseph's beautiful forgiving spirit was his firm belief that God is in control. In Genesis 45, Joseph looked back on his trial of mistreatment and there was no trace of resentment or self-pity in his words. Instead, he said again and again that God was in control of all the circumstances of his life. Genesis 45:5—" . . . God sent me . . ." Genesis 45:7—" . . . God sent me . . ." Genesis 45:8—"It was not you who sent me here, but God." In nine other places in chapter 45, Joseph emphasized that it was God who made him a success as prime minister of Egypt. Joseph saw himself as a man sent by God and made by God, and it was Joseph's trust in the sovereignty of God that enabled him to forgive all the people who had mistreated him.

The same is true of your life and mine. Even when mistreated, you and I can know that God is sovereign, he is in control of our lives. Because God is the Lord of our lives, we know he either willed or allowed our circumstances. We can trust him, believing he will weave all our hurts into his good plan. We can know that, like Joseph, we are people who have been sent by God and made by God. He has been using all the circumstances in our lives to shape us and conform us into the image of Jesus Christ.

Ultimately, the issue of mistreatment forces us to face this question: Do we believe God is in control? Do we believe he either wills or allows everything that happens in our lives? If we really believe that, we become unstoppable, because we refuse to let past disappointments shape our future. Because we believe God is in control and that he is unlimited, we believe the future is limitless as well. Regardless of how the past has hurt us, we know who holds the future, and we are excited and optimistic about tomorrow.

Clarence Jordan was a godly optimist, a man of positive power. In 1940, Jordan went to rural Georgia with a Ph.D. in agriculture, another Ph.D. in New Testament Greek, and a burden for the poor. There he founded Koinonia Farm, a place where disadvantaged people, most of them black, could learn to be more effective farmers and could sell the products of their labor. It was a place that ministered to both the physical and spiritual needs of its people.

Throughout his first few years as director of Koinonia Farm, Jordan faced continual mistreatment and prejudice. He was cursed and spat upon by people in the town. The tires of his pickup were slashed repeatedly. The produce from the farm was boycotted.

One night in 1954, a Ku Klux Klan "posse" arrived at the farm. Hooded men erected a burning cross in the middle of the yard, then torched the sheds and barns and riddled Jordan's home with bullets while he huddled on the floor. He recognized many of the Klansmen's voices. Some were members of the church Jordan attended in town.

The next morning, Jordan arose early, went to his field, and surveyed the damage. All the tender young shoots of the spring planting had been trampled. With a whispered prayer, Jordan lifted his hoe, bent his back, and began to plant. He was beginning again.

While he worked, a car pulled up and a man from the newspaper office got out and walked over, grinning. Jordan acknowledged the man's presence, then went back to his labor. He had heard the newspaper man's voice during the Klan raid, too. The man looked around at the burned buildings and trampled crops, then said, "Well, you've got your two Ph.D.s and you've been here for fourteen years. All you've got to show for it is a few piles of ashes. Just how successful do you think you've been, Mr. Jordan?"

Jordan looked up from his hoeing. "About as successful as the cross of Jesus," he said. Then he went back to work.

Today, Koinonia Farm continues to minister to physical and spiritual needs in Georgia. Even fire and bullets could not stop Clarence Jordan because Jordan knew that God was in control. Koinonia Farm looked like a failure—as big a failure as the cross. But just as death could not hold Jesus Christ, Clarence Jordan knew that the Klan could not stop him. He would not stop working and risking. With the power of faith and a positive attitude, Jordan would take hold of the future and shape it into something beautiful.

There's a young man who has something to say about a positive attitude, and you've probably heard of him. His name is Beaver Cleaver. A few years ago, when my son Nathan was a pre-schooler, he and I used to watch "Leave It to Beaver" reruns together once a week on my day off. Every episode of that show was built around a moral theme, such as honesty, courage, or perseverance. After each show, Nathan and I would discuss the moral of the episode—how Beaver should have ignored the bad advice of his friends or how he should have obeyed his parents or how he should have told the truth.

In one episode, Beaver's friend Richard came over to visit. As the boys were talking in Beaver's room, Richard said, "Hey, Beav, I heard this word today—'optimist.' You know what an 'optimist' is?"

"I think so," Beaver replied. "An optimist is a guy who falls off a ninety-story building and halfway down he says to himself, 'So far, so good.' "

Well, that's one definition of an optimist. But I want to suggest a much deeper and more meaningful definition. I believe God is calling you and me to a kind of "godly optimism" which is rooted in a realistic understanding of the evils of this world, which understands that the systems and dynamics of our culture are under satanic domination, which acknowledges that injustice and mistreatment are to be expected in this life—yet which does not despair, give up, or become embittered. How, in the face of all the world's evil, can we keep an optimistic outlook? Because Jesus is the King, God is the Judge, and all that is now wrong will one day be made right. One day, all wounds will be healed, all tears will be wiped away, all sorrow will be no more.

An interviewer once asked Billy Graham why he is an optimist. He replied, "Because I've read the last chapter of the Book." Billy Graham knows how history will end, and so do you and I. We know that, even though evil reigns today, God will have the final victory. As Martin Luther proclaims in that stirring hymn, "A Mighty Fortress Is Our God":

"The body they may kill,
God's truth abideth still:
His kingdom is forever."

Elizabeth Morris is a living example of the sovereign power of God to bring good out of terrible mistreatment. Several years ago, just before

Christmas, she received a phone call from the hospital. Her eighteen-year-old son Ted had been killed in a head-on collision. The driver of the other car received only minor lacerations. He had three times the legal limit of alcohol in his bloodstream. His name was Tommy.

Elizabeth and her husband Frank were devastated. The promise of their son's life had been destroyed in an instant by a drunk. Elizabeth and Frank went to the courtroom where the young man was arraigned on a charge of manslaughter. They were sickened to hear him plead not guilty.

In her grief, Elizabeth wrestled with the question of God's sovereignty. How could God be in control? How could he be loving? How could God allow this to happen to her son? How could anything good come out of such a horrible loss? It seemed so horribly unfair that her own son should die and Tommy should live. "If I ever see him walking across the street," she once told her husband, "I'll run him down!"

Weeks dragged into months as Tommy's case went through postponement after postponement. The young man remained free, never having spent a night in jail, and he still carried a valid driver's license. Elizabeth's hatred intensified to a point where she could think and talk of nothing else but seeing Tommy punished. Finally the sentence was handed down: five years probation. Elizabeth was outraged. The man who had killed her son would go free.

During this time, God was at work on Elizabeth's heart. She began to hear lines from the Bible playing in her mind: "Forgive, not seven times, but seventy times seven. . . . Love your enemies. . . . Do not take revenge." She wrestled with conflicting impulses—the desire to forgive warred against the desire for revenge. The battle continued.

One day she sat in the auditorium of the high school where Ted had graduated. As part of his probation, Tommy was required to speak to the students at a special assembly organized by Mothers Against Drunk Driving. Elizabeth wanted to hear what Tommy had to say. "I want to tell you about the night I killed Ted Morris," he began, a look of anguish on his face. "I got drunk, I got in a car, and I killed a guy who was just about the same age as a lot of you kids. When they told me Ted had died, I couldn't stop crying. To think of all the people I hurt—the truth is, they should've put me in prison."

Elizabeth couldn't believe what she was hearing. All along she had pictured Tommy as a monster without a conscience. Now she saw him as a pitiful young man, drowning in guilt.

Over the coming weeks, Elizabeth made a point of getting to know this young man. Day by day, her feelings wavered between sympathy and revulsion. Sometimes she would smell alcohol on his breath and the old hatred would revive. Yet there was an air of sorrow and tragedy about Tommy that tugged at her heart. "How much are you drinking?" she asked him one time.

"I start drinking every day after work. I put a pillow on the phone to keep it from ringing, then I drink until I fall asleep."

Eventually, Tommy's drinking led him to break probation and he was forced to go to jail. When

Elizabeth discovered he had no visitors, she went to see him. Sitting across from Tommy, she felt a wave of compassion come over her. It didn't make sense. *This is the man who killed Ted*, she kept telling herself. Yet she could feel the last dregs of her hatred draining away. They talked for a while, and finally Tommy said, "Mrs. Morris, I'm so sorry about Ted. Would you—could you please forgive me?"

"I forgive you, Tommy," she replied. "But I want you to forgive me, too."

"Forgive you? For what?"

"For hating you."

In time, Elizabeth came to understand Tommy's troubled background and his desperate desire to break his alcohol addiction. She also remembered Jesus said not only to forgive your enemies, but to do good to them. So she began doing good to Tommy. She visited him, encouraged him in his recovery from alcoholism, and explained to him how Jesus Christ could give him a completely new life.

Tommy was sometimes released in the Morrises' custody so that they could take him to different schools, where he gave his talks to teenagers, or to the Morrises' church on Sundays. On one trip, they were driving near the church when Tommy said, "I was reading in my Bible that a Christian is supposed to be baptized. I think I'm ready." Because the Morrises' church allowed laypeople to baptize, they drove directly to the church and Frank took Tommy into the baptistry. It was the same church where Frank had performed the same sacrament for his then-eleven-year-old son Ted. As Elizabeth watched, Frank Morris baptized Tommy.

After Tommy was paroled, Elizabeth and Frank often invited him to their home. He hasn't had a drink since he left prison. Tommy likes to help Elizabeth and Frank, cutting their grass or doing other chores. When Tommy visits the Morrises, he feels like he's home.

Elizabeth was able to forgive Tommy because she ultimately came to accept—despite her grief and her anger—that God is sovereign. She discovered that God can bring good out of her deepest hurts, even something as painful as the death of a son.[2]

God is in control of all the circumstances of our lives. That fact gives us the power to live as positive people in a negative world. Because God is limitless, our future is unlimited as well. We have the power to break the chains of the past. My prayer is that you and I become the kind of people who are excited about the future, secure in the fact that our destiny is in the powerful hands of a loving God.

Notes

1. Bruce Larson, *There's a Lot More to Health Than Not Being Sick* (Waco, Texas: Word Books, 1981, 1984), p. 101.

2. Elizabeth Morris, "Seventy Times Seven," *Guideposts*, vol. 40, no. 11, January 1976, pp. 2-6.

CHAPTER NINE

Somebody's Watching You

The early years of little Billy Dukenfield's life were years of pain. Billy was born into the grimy, hard-scrabble environment of central Philadelphia in the 1880s. His father was a saloon-keeper, a heavy drinker with a violent temper. His mother was a bitter woman with a scathing tongue. Billy's home was a tiny walk-up apartment over the bar.

Billy's relationship with his father was distant and marked by frequent beatings. Yet this boy was very devoted to his mother. There was one consolation in Billy's life, and that was Christmastime. It was not the meager presents he looked forward to. Rather it was that special kind of family togetherness that Christmas brings, when old wounds and family struggles were temporarily forgotten and it seemed there was love in his home—if only for a little while.

But this little boy's love of Christmas died because of something that happened when he was eight years old. As a grown man, he recalled, "I saved up some money carrying ice in Philadelphia, and I was going to buy my mother a copper-bottomed clothes boiler for Christmas. I hid the money in a brown crock in the coal bin, but my father found the crock. He stole the money and got drunk. Ever since then, I've remembered nobody on Christmas, and I want nobody to remember me."

Embittered and lonely, Billy left home at the age of eleven, supporting himself with odd jobs while teaching himself how to juggle and tell jokes. He had no use for God or sentiment and lived his life as an agnostic. He eventually graduated to the vaudeville stage, where he substituted laughter and applause for love. Remembering the example of his alcoholic father, he at first avoided alcohol—though he purchased the friendship of fellow vaudevillians by buying them drinks. Soon he began drinking as well, eventually acquiring a quart-a-day whiskey habit. As so often happens to the children of alcoholics, Billy both hated and embraced the pattern of his father's alcoholism.

The childhood pain and mistreatment suffered by little Billy—so poignantly exemplified by the theft of his Christmas savings when he was eight years old—set a pattern for his adulthood: Loneliness. Alcoholism. Agnosticism.

A final irony was that this man, who had hated Christmas since boyhood, died on Christmas Day,

1946, in Hollywood, California. He had made a name for himself on the vaudeville stage, on national radio, and in motion pictures such as *Never Give a Sucker an Even Break* and *My Little Chickadee*—and the name he made for himself was W. C. Fields.

Just before his death, a friend visited Fields in his hospital room and found him reading a Bible. "Do my eyes deceive me," exclaimed the friend, "or is that really a Bible in your hands?"

Fields's typically wry reply: "Just looking for loopholes." I hope W. C. Fields found his "loophole"—or more precisely, I hope he discovered the saving grace of God before his death. Only God knows. But, to me, Fields's early life is symbolic of a very common hurt—the hurt of childhood mistreatment. I've spent hundreds of hours counseling people with broken self-esteem and painful memories due to childhood mistreatment by relatives, teachers, or peers. I'm convinced there is a wounded child within most of us.

Dick Gregory knows that kind of pain. He was seven years old, sitting in the back of his grammar school classroom in inner-city St. Louis. His little desk sat in the center of a chalk circle—the troublemaker's seat. His teacher considered him unteachable—"a little black boy who squirmed in his idiot's seat and made noises and poked the kids around him," as Gregory later recalled, "because he wanted someone to know he was there." He was poor, fatherless, and usually hungry.

It was a Thursday in the early 1940s. The teacher stood before the class and asked each child how much money his or her father would give to the

Community Chest. The children were to bring the money to class the following Monday for the teacher to collect. As she opened her book and called each child by name, little Richard Gregory decided he was going to buy himself a daddy. He had almost three dollars in dimes and quarters in his pocket from shining shoes and selling papers. He was going to pledge it all.

The teacher called out name after name, and each child announced his or her daddy's donation—a dollar, two dollars, two and a half. Richard waited for his name to be called. But when she finally closed her book, the teacher had called every name but his. Richard raised his hand. "You forgot me," he said. "My daddy said he'd give—"

"Sit down, Richard. You're disturbing the class."

"My daddy said he'd give—fifteen dollars!"

The teacher glared at the little boy. "We are collecting this money for you and your kind, Richard Gregory. If your daddy can give fifteen dollars you have no business being on relief."

The little boy's throat tightened. "I got it right now. My daddy gave it to me to turn in today. He said—"

"And furthermore, Richard, we all know you don't have a daddy!" All the children turned to stare at him, some snickering, some pitying. Helene Tucker, the little girl he had a crush on, began to cry for him. He couldn't see the children's faces very well, because he had begun to cry too.

"Sit down, Richard," ordered the teacher. But Richard didn't sit down. "Where are you going, Richard?"

Dick Gregory later wrote, "I walked out of school that day, and for a long time I didn't go back. . . . There was shame there."[1] Shame—one of the most awful feelings in the world. Even after the passage of decades, our faces can still burn with shame at the memory of childhood mistreatment.

So often, as I've watched the pain of early youth stab at an adult heart, I've been keenly aware that childhood in real life does not always match up with the images we recall from "Father Knows Best" or "Leave It to Beaver." You may not have known the kind of wise, evenhanded father we see on black-and-white TV reruns—the gray-templed dad with the guiding hand and sage advice, taking you fishing and to Sunday school and bailing you out of your problems in the nick of time. You may have had a parent who rejected you or a friend who betrayed you. You may have been shunned or hurt by your peers. The good news is you don't have to be chained down by the past.

There's a young woman named Joan who understands what it means to move beyond the mistreatment of her early past. Raised by parents who had no use for God, Joan was blind from birth. Her parents were unable to accept her handicap. They bitterly resented the hand "fate" had dealt them in giving them a blind child. While Joan's older sister was praised, pampered, and given every advantage in life, Joan was shunted aside from her parents' affection. They frequently reminded her how limited she was by her blindness, how she could never achieve the things sighted people achieve. Once, when Joan mentioned her hopes of someday having a career or getting married, her parents laughed at her. When she talked about going to college, they said, "We're not putting out good money for an education that will never be used!"

Though deeply bruised in her self-image, Joan was determined to prove her parents wrong. She dedicated herself to succeeding as a blind young woman in a sighted world. She taught herself Braille, excelled in her high school studies, and finally achieved a full scholarship to a major state university. It was there she met Pastor Glenn.

Pastor Glenn, the campus chaplain, saw something in Joan, an aura of strength mingled with deep hurt, that led him to take a special interest in her. He was fascinated by the paradox of this young woman who seemed so fragile and lonely within her world of darkness, yet who was so powerfully driven to achieve success.

Because Joan's roommate went home most weekends, Saturdays and Sundays were especially lonely for Joan. Pastor Glenn found Sunday afternoons a good time to visit her at the dorm. As they talked together, Pastor Glenn began to understand how deeply Joan had been hurt by the pattern of mistreatment in her childhood and adolescence. Week by week, he shared with her about the loving Father he knew, a Father who accepts all our weakness and pain, then transforms it into something beautiful.

He opened his Bible to many Scripture passages during their talks, but the one that meant the most to her was Romans 8:28—"And we know that God causes all things to work together for good to those who love God, to those who are called according to

His purpose" (NASB). The moment she realized God could transform her pain into his good and weave it into his plan was the moment light suddenly flooded her life with meaning and purpose. As Pastor Glenn prayed with her, she committed her life to Jesus.

Shortly before Joan was scheduled to return home for spring vacation, she and Pastor Glenn talked about her new life in Christ. A moment of silence elapsed between them and a wistful expression crossed Joan's face. "Pastor Glenn," she said at last, "if I could have one wish, do you know what it would be?"

Inwardly, Pastor Glenn surmised that her wish would be to have the gift of sight. He was mistaken.

"I would wish," she continued, "that my parents had been Christians so they could have taught me that my blindness could be used for God's good."

Joan had made a big first step beyond bitterness, self-pity, and the drivenness that so often accompanies broken self-esteem. She still has many more steps to take, but she is on her way.

What about you?

You may have had a painful childhood, too, but you are an adult now. What happened in the past is dead. Now you are responsible for the present—and the future. What will you do with today and tomorrow? How will you shape the time that is in your hands? Will you break the cycle of mistreatment or will you pass on your hurt to others? Will you continue in the old, failed patterns of the past or are you ready to build a new life for yourself, a life free of bitterness and resentment? And what are you teaching your children and the others around you who are watching your life? What are you teaching them by your response to mistreatment?

A recent psychological study determined that there are three principal ways in which children learn at home. First, about 7 percent of what a child learns is acquired verbally. We try to teach our children how to live through words such as, "You ought to love God. You ought to love your brother. You ought to obey your parents." It's good that we try to verbally instruct our children, but we need to remember that our words comprise only 7 percent of their learning experience. Secondly, about 18 percent of what our children learn from us comes through shared experiences—going fishing or to a ballgame together, or trips to the zoo or a museum. Finally, 75 percent of what our children learn from us comes through modeling, through their observation of our living, active example.

Our children watch how Dad treats Mom, how Mom responds to Dad, how both parents treat the children. They absorb their parents' attitudes to the minor annoyances in life, to the major crises, to the rude driver in the next lane, to the abrasive neighbor, or the friend or relative who overstays his welcome. Children are like sponges and they soak up every stray word or action we parents carelessly throw off—and their absorption of our actions, whether for good or ill, forms 75 percent of their learning process in the home. We have enormous power to shape the minds and attitudes of our children.

We would do well to ask ourselves, "What kind of an example am I? Do I model the kind of positive encouragement people inwardly hunger for? Do I model a positive yes-attitude to life? Do the children who are watching my life see a model of forgiveness—or of bitterness? When opportunities come my way disguised as crises, how do I respond? Am I aware, as I daily interact with my children, that the attitudes I want to teach them are more often caught than taught? That what I do as I demonstrate my faith and character is much more important than what I say?"

You and I have an enormous responsibility that is far too easy to pass off lightly. Our neighbors, our co-workers, our friends, our family, and most of all our children are watching us, observing how we function under fire. Whether you like it or not, you are living out your life in a fishbowl. Somebody is watching you. What is that person learning from you about a godly, therapeutic response to mistreatment?

Two people who take this responsibility seriously are John and Christine Haggai. A number of years ago, the Haggais had a son. In his mother's womb, little John, Jr., was a perfectly formed, healthy baby waiting to be born. But something went tragically, needlessly wrong during John's birth.

The Haggais had gone to one of the most respected obstetricians in the nation for their baby's prenatal care and delivery. Yet this doctor had just experienced a personal tragedy, and he had gone to a whiskey bottle for consolation. Then he delivered John and Christine's little boy. The result was a baby with several broken bones, a dislocated leg, a forceps-damaged skull, and brain hemorrhaging.

During the first few months of the baby's life, specialists predicted he would not see his first birthday. But this baby confounded the specialists.

Throughout his first two years, he required special feedings at three-hour intervals around the clock. Each feeding took an hour to prepare and administer. John and Christine rarely got more than two hours of uninterrupted sleep in those first two years.

Before the baby's birth, Christine was considered one of the leading Christian singers in the country. After his birth, she stayed at home, humming lullabies to her crippled baby boy. Reflecting on his family's years of trial, John Haggai now says,

> John Edmund, Jr., our little son, lived more than twenty years. We rejoice that he committed his heart and life to Jesus Christ and gave evidence of a genuine concern for the things of the Lord. I attribute his commitment to Jesus Christ and his wonderful disposition to the sparkling radiance of an emotionally mature, Christ-centered mother who has mastered the discipline of living one day at a time. Never have I—nor has anyone else—heard a word of complaint from her. The people who know her concur that at thirty-five years of age and after having been subjected to more grief than many people twice her age, she possessed sparkle that would be the envy of any high school senior and the radiance and charm for which any debutante would gladly give a fortune.[2]

Don't you want to have that kind of influence on your children and on the people around you? Don't you want to be able to transform the mistreatment you have suffered into something beautiful in the lives of others? I do.

I have a fourteen-year-old friend named Jason Eisenman who recently wrote down his thoughts on the powerful influence his adoptive parents have had on his life. He writes,

> Once when I was a lot younger I watched a television show on abortion. I saw how many thousands of women were aborting their babies before they were born. I remember how glad I was that my biological mother chose to carry me and my twin brother Josh to full term and give birth. Then she let us be adopted into a wonderful family. I might not even be here today, except that my biological mother loved me enough to let me be born. And my new family loved me enough to make a wonderful home for me.
>
> A lot of people think adoption is a bad thing. They think maybe the parents that adopt you wouldn't love you as much as their own kids. Sometimes this may be true, but in my family it is not.
>
> When my parents adopted me, they took a big risk. They knew in my biological family there was a problem called dyslexia, a severe reading disability. They also knew there was diabetes in my biological family. I was born with one foot turned in, and I had to have surgery to correct an indentation in my skull. My parents knew they would need to give me special attention. Knowing all this, they still wanted Josh and me, even though twins

are twice the work. My mom and dad didn't care that Josh and I were black and they were white. They loved us just the way we were.

One good thing about adoption is I always know I was really loved and wanted, because I was chosen. When I get to be 18, I know I could look for my biological parents, but I would not. I already have a loving and caring mom and dad. Adoption is the greatest gift in life to me.

My young friend Jason is adopted—but he's fortunate, more fortunate than many children who live with the moms and dads who gave them birth but who fail to model a healthy, positive, forgiving response to the trials of this life.

You and I have so much power at our fingertips, power to exemplify a godly, therapeutic response to mistreatment, power to mold and encourage our children, power to attract others to God. We also have the power to continue the cycle of bitterness and mistreatment, to destroy the self-esteem of our children, to rob God of his honor. Someone is watching you to see what choices you will make. Those choices are never made in isolation. The effect of the way you respond to disappointment, to trials, to mistreatment, is sure to ripple out into the lives of others.

Many years ago there were two altar boys serving in two Catholic churches thousands of miles from each other. One boy was born in 1892 in Eastern Europe, in the little Croatian village of Kumrovec. The other was born just three years later in a small town in Illinois. Though they lived very separate lives in very different parts of the world, these two altar boys had almost identical experiences. Each boy was given the opportunity to assist his parish priest in the service of Communion. Ironically, each boy, while handling the communion cup, accidentally spilled some of the wine on the carpet. There the similarities end.

The priest in the Eastern European church, seeing the purple stain on the carpet, slapped the little altar boy hard across the face and shouted, "Clumsy oaf! Leave the altar!" That little boy grew up to become an atheist and a Communist. He was the strongman dictator of Yugoslavia from 1943 to 1980. His name was Josip Broz Tito.

The priest in the church in Illinois, upon seeing the stain near the altar, knelt down to the little boy's level, looked him tenderly in the eyes and said, "It's all right, son. You'll do better next time. You'll be a fine priest for God someday." That little boy grew up to become Bishop Fulton J. Sheen, a man whose speaking and writing has touched millions of hearts for God.

Two lives impacted in very different ways—one by the power of positive affirmation and forgiveness, the other by crippling words and a blow to the face. The small choices you and I make, whether for good or ill, become enormously magnified in the lives of those around us. Whenever you suffer mistreatment, you are given the opportunity to influence others by the example of your response. We don't dare let this opportunity pass without using it to transform our mistreatment into something good in the lives of others.

Notes

1. Dick Gregory with Robert Lipsyte, *Nigger: An Autobiography* (New York: Pocket Books, 1965), pp. 30-32.

2. John Haggai, *How to Win Over Worry* (Grand Rapids: Zondervan Publishing House, 1976), pp. 95-96.

CHAPTER TEN

Freedom from the Tyranny of Self

Throughout the 1920s, '30s, and '40s, Kathleen Thompson Norris dominated the best-seller lists with such romantic novels as *Belle-Mere*, *Shining Windows*, and *Storm House*. Few of her millions of readers, however, knew of the tragedy that marked her earlier life. At the age of nineteen, Kathleen suffered the double tragedy of losing both her mother and father within a month of each other. Although she found happiness again the next year when she married novelist Charles Norris and subsequently gave birth to two lovely daughters and a little boy, tragedy was soon to strike once more.

Within one three-week period, both of Kathleen's little girls died of influenza and pneumonia.

Devastated by her loss, Kathleen convinced Charles they should move from San Francisco to New York City and start a new life. There, she threw herself into her writing, completing three new novels during her first year in New York. While her writing met with critical acclaim and commercial success, she could not escape a nagging sense of unhappiness and emptiness left by the loss of her "little darlings."

During this time, a friend told Kathleen of an "unsanctioned" baby—the child of an unwed mother—being cared for at Bellevue Hospital. Kathleen went to the hospital and fell in love with the baby at first sight. That same day, she had adoption papers drawn. After two weeks of hospital care, the baby would be hers to take home.

Kathleen visited the infant every day. When two weeks had nearly passed, she was told the baby had developed an infection and would need to stay a couple days longer. When she arrived before noon the next day, however, she was met by the head nurse. "I don't know quite how to tell you this, Mrs. Norris, but—"

Kathleen could see the terrible news in the nurse's eyes: The baby had died.

The nurse put her arm around Kathleen's shoulders and continued to talk, easing her into a chair. Kathleen barely heard the nurse's next words. "People are born and people die in this hospital every day," the nurse said, "but I never get used to the job of breaking bad news. Why, at this very moment, there's a little boy in the next room whose mother died not half an hour ago. He doesn't know it yet, poor thing, and now somebody has to tell him

that he's all alone in the world. I don't suppose—"
The nurse hesitated.

"What?" Kathleen looked up suddenly. "Do you want me to tell the boy his mother died?"

"It was a foolish thought," said the nurse. "I had no right to ask—"

"Actually, I think it's a very good idea," Kathleen said. "I would like to tell him."

After drying her eyes and composing herself, she went with the nurse to the doorway of a nearby waiting room. Then, with a smile and a casual air, she strode into the next room and met a worried-looking eight-year-old boy. "Well, hello there! What's your name?" she asked brightly.

"Billy."

"Well, Billy, I'm Mrs. Norris. I'm very hungry, but I simply hate to eat alone. Aren't you hungry, too? There's a nice place to eat just on the next block. Would you like to have lunch with me, Billy?"

"I don't know," the boy said dubiously. "My mother might wake up, and she's gonna want to see me. The nurse promised to call me if she—"

"Well, I'll tell the nurse where we'll be. Then, if your mother wakes up—" she paused to steady her voice—"if she wakes up, the nurse will call us at the restaurant."

"Well—Okay."

Kathleen and Billy got along fine through lunch. She even persuaded the boy to go with her to the hotel where she lived. There, she showed him some books that belonged to her own little boy. Outside, the sky was just beginning to darken. Billy said, "I think I should be going now. My mother may be waking up."

Kathleen knew the time had come. "Billy," she said slowly, "there's something I have to tell you." A few hours earlier, he would have learned of his mother's death from a stranger. Now he heard it from a friend. He cried himself to sleep in the arms of his new friend. And in the coming years, he grew up in the home of this friend.

Billy grew up to become Bill Norris, a well-known newspaper reporter on the West Coast, and Kathleen loved him as her own son. Though she never forgot the particular sting of each of her tragic losses—her parents, her little girls, and the baby she loved but never took home—Kathleen Norris experienced the healing joy of reaching out to another hurting soul in the midst of her own sorrow. She discovered how to transform her hurt by reaching beyond herself and her own hurts, by touching the hurts of a grieving little boy.

That's the lesson you and I need to learn as we endeavor to move beyond the hurt of mistreatment. When we've suffered hurt, there is tremendous therapeutic value in finding a cause greater than ourselves to which we can commit. If we have no greater cause than seeking our own happiness, we will ultimately become absorbed and obsessed with self. When a self-absorbed person suffers mistreatment, self-pity inevitably follows. We will never be free of the tyranny of the past until we are free of the tyranny of self.

There is a young man named Brent who has learned how to move beyond mistreatment by transcending self and reaching out to others. As a child, he was repeatedly battered by his father. He left home in his mid-teens, worked hard, and managed to accumulate ten thousand dollars in savings. At age twenty, he married a woman ten years his senior. A week after their marriage, she cleaned out his bank account and disappeared. By his late twenties, Brent was an angry young man—distrustful and wary in his relationships, unhappy with his life, pessimistic about the future.

He read various books on "self-fulfillment" which encouraged him to "get in touch" with himself. He decided he needed some counseling to guide him on his "journey inward," so he consulted a psychiatrist, a psychologist, an astrologer, and counselors from churches ranging from Catholic to Lutheran to Scientology. Despite all the advice he received, he just kept getting more and more confused.

Finally, one of the pastors who was counseling Brent asked him if he had a personal relationship with Jesus Christ. Brent said no, he felt completely cut off from God. So the pastor asked if he wanted to turn control of his life over to Jesus Christ. Brent said he did, so the two of them prayed together and a revolution occurred in Brent's mind and heart. He became involved in the church, meeting with a small group of believers in a "care group." They prayed and studied the Bible together and shared their hurts and struggles with each other. There he found that other people had problems and painful memories, too. He was amazed to find they wanted and needed his insights, his prayers, his compassion, just as he needed theirs. Soon, he was involved in several areas of the church ministry, including an outreach to Southeast Asian refugees.

Through these experiences, Brent discovered that his greatest joy lay not in some introspective process of self-discovery, but in rousing himself to serve others. Today, Brent is living proof that one of the best ways to overcome a past filled with mistreatment is servanthood, reaching beyond yourself. Certainly, pastoral and clinical counseling is valuable and often necessary to finding emotional wholeness. But until Brent became willing to focus on the needs and hurts of others and until he became actively involved in meeting those needs, he remained mired in a muddle of introspection.

One saying of Christ is recorded in all four Gospels, Matthew, Mark, Luke, and John: "Whoever finds his life will lose it, and whoever loses his life for my sake will find it." I've seen the truth of that statement proved over and over again: those who try to "find" themselves, who try to get "into" themselves, almost always end up losing themselves by sinking into a morass of confusion, alienation, and self-pity. But those who get out of themselves, who "lose" themselves in service to God and to others, almost invariably find themselves. They discover new strengths and abilities, new levels of understanding, new facets of character deep within themselves. Most of all, they find they simply have no time for self-pity.

With that as our focus, we can see that the mistreatment we have suffered is not just a random, meaningless wound. Rather, that mistreatment becomes a resource we can use to help heal the hurts of those around us. We actually find healing in our own souls as we make our own experiences— both our pain and our joy—available to others to help them gain insight and healing for their hurts.

Moreover, the mistreatment you and I have suffered gives us the authority and authenticity to help others who are hurting. Our painful experiences enable us to speak as people who have lived not in an ivory tower, but in the trenches of life. As Henri Nouwen observed in his book *The Wounded Healer*, "Who can save a child from a burning house without taking the risk of being hurt by the flames? Who can listen to a story of loneliness and despair without taking the risk of experiencing similar pains in his own heart and even losing his precious peace of mind? In short: Who can take away suffering without entering it? The great illusion . . . is to think that man can be led out of the desert by someone who has never been there."[1]

Because you have been to the desert of mistreatment, you have received a great gift. You now have the gift of empathy. You know what it is like to be mistreated. That gives you the right and the authority to talk to others who have been deeply hurt by life. You have a depth of understanding and insight that few others have. By using your experience of mistreatment instead of simply trying to escape it, you can find the truest form of emotional wholeness and freedom. You can witness the miraculous transformation of hurt into healing.

Over a hundred years ago, an incident occurred in a Scottish seaside inn that symbolizes how the ugly events in this life can be transformed into something marvelous. A group of fishermen were relaxing in the inn after a long day at sea. They were trading fish stories, as fishermen do, while their meal was being prepared. As a serving maid was walking past the fishermen's table with a pot of tea, one of the men made a sweeping gesture to describe the size of the fish he claimed to have caught. His hand collided with the teapot and sent it crashing against the whitewashed wall, where its contents left an irregular brown splotch.

Standing nearby, the innkeeper surveyed the damage. "That stain will never come out," he said in dismay. "The whole wall will have to be repainted."

"Perhaps not."

All eyes turned to the stranger who had just spoken. "What do you mean?" asked the innkeeper.

"Let me work with the stain," said the stranger, standing up from his table in the corner. "If my work meets your approval, you won't need to repaint the wall."

The innkeeper nodded dubiously.

The stranger picked up a box he had with him and went to the wall. Opening the box, he withdrew pencils, brushes, and some glass jars of linseed oil and pigment. Then he went to work. He began to sketch lines around the stain and fill it in here and there with dabs of color and swashes of shading. Soon a picture began to emerge. The random splashes of tea had become a medium of artistic expression, rendered into the image of a stag with a magnificent rack of antlers. At the bottom of the picture, the man inscribed his signature. Then he paid for his meal and left.

The innkeeper was stunned when he examined the artist's signature. "Do you know who that man was?" he said in amazement. "The signature reads 'E. H. Landseer'!" Indeed, they had been visited by the well-known painter of wildlife, Sir Edwin Landseer. He had demonstrated what is possible when an ugly stain is not simply erased or covered over but is transformed into a thing of beauty. And that is exactly what God wants to do with all the stain-like events that enter your life and mine.

I've known scores of people who have seen this kind of transformation in their own lives. For a time during their trial of mistreatment, their faith was stretched to the limit. Yet a few weeks, months, or years after their trial, they came to me and said, "Ron, it's so clear now what God was doing. I can see how he has woven my hurt into a beautiful new pattern." That is what God wants to do with your trial of unfair treatment. Your life is God's art form, his handiwork, and the creative process of fashioning your life into a pattern of beauty goes on and on, as long as you live.

Let's return to Genesis for one final look at the life of Joseph. There, in the concluding chapter of the book, we see that Joseph's lifelong goal was to release all bitterness, to forgive all wrongs, to live free—and ultimately, to die free. In Genesis 50:20, Joseph tells his brothers who so many years before had sold him into slavery, "You intended to harm me, but God intended it for good. . . ." That's the 50:20 Principle, the principle that governed Joseph's life, that determined his response to mistreatment, that enabled him to live free of resentment.

Then, just a few verses down the page, we read verse 26: "So Joseph died at the age of a hundred and ten. And after they embalmed him, he was placed in a coffin in Egypt." That's the end of the book of Genesis, and the end of the story of Joseph—but not the end of Joseph's legacy. His positive, loving, forgiving spirit lives on in all those who allow God to transform their trials of mistreatment into something beautiful. God molded the medium of his life into an art form, a masterpiece of grace and forgiveness that speaks to us across thousands of years. Joseph's legacy, the 50:20 Principle, can live on in you and me.

On his syndicated radio broadcast, Dr. James Dobson recently described his father's spiritual legacy. He said that when he went to select the headstone for his father's grave, he never had to wonder what words to put on it. He knew exactly what the stone should say. The resting place of Dr. Dobson's father is marked only by his father's name and the words, "He prayed." I imagine the tomb of Joseph could have been marked by such words as "He forgave."

What sort of legacy are you leaving behind? What words would sum up the kind of life you have lived? Words like those which describe Joseph? Or words such as "Victim of mistreatment" or "Died in bitterness" or "Unforgiving to the end"? To grow old and die without bitterness is one of the greatest legacies we can leave our loved ones, our children, and our grandchildren.

"All the while I thought I was learning how to live," Leonardo da Vinci once said, "when I was really learning how to die." What was true for

Leonardo da Vinci is true for you and me. All of life—everything we experience, suffer, enjoy, think, and are—is pointed toward eternity. What sort of preparation are you and I making for it?

Joseph died at peace with others, at peace with himself, and at peace with God. What better way to live and die than this! When my body is beyond healing, I want to leave it with a healed spirit, with healed memories, with whole and loving relationships. I want to be able to say to anyone who has mistreated me, "I forgive you. You meant it for evil, but God has transformed it into his good." That's the 50:20 Principle at work even at the end of life. I want to imprint it on my heart and live it out every day of my life.

By our example, we are teaching this tired and hurting world that the human spirit, empowered by the life-giving Spirit of God, need not be conquered by mistreatment. We are living by the 50:20 Principle, "You meant it for evil, but God has used it for good." So long as you can say those words from your heart, you will never be a victim. You will be free.

One woman wrote several lines I will never forget, words about her own struggle to find freedom from bitterness. She spoke of the times she had felt unwanted, unloved, and friendless, the times she ached to share her love with someone else, but no one was there. Through it all, she was thankful for the saving love of Jesus in her life, and she concluded,

"Lord Jesus, you have saved me from
   Hell's black abyss.

Now save me from the tyranny of bitterness."

The tyranny of bitterness. Throughout his life, Joseph had experienced many forms of tyranny, but one form that had no hold on him was the tyranny of bitterness. May the same be true of you and me.

Emotional wholeness is not a destination. It's a journey. My friend, you and I are on that journey. We are learning, building inner strength, preparing to meet the challenges of the future—and there will be future challenges. In this life, we will have trials of mistreatment. It's a natural part of life.

But there is a place beyond mistreatment, and that place is in eternity. When you arrive at that place, you will be able to look back on all the evil events in your life and there will be no more pain in those memories. For then, at last, you will be able to see the complete design. You will see how the pattern of your hurt has been interwoven with the pattern of all those millions of others who have suffered unjustly.

And then you will understand.

Notes

1. Henri J. M. Nouwen, *The Wounded Healer: Ministry in Contemporary Society* (Garden City, N.Y.: Doubleday & Company, 1972), pp. 72-73.

Study Guide

*This study guide was developed to help readers better utilize the important concepts in **Mistreated**. It connects key insights from the book with selected passages from the Bible. Important thoughts from each chapter of the book are excerpted and then paired with Scripture portions related to the ideas under review. Discussion questions follow, designed to encourage readers to make full use of the strategies contained in the book.*

To make best use of this study guide, we suggest the following steps:

1. Pray for God's wisdom and guidance as you begin.

2. *Read carefully the chapter to be studied.*

3. *Place in context each excerpt featured in the study guide by referring back to the page from which the excerpt was taken (the page number is noted in the guide).*

4. *Read carefully the Scripture passages that accompany each excerpt.*

5. *Use the discussion questions as guides to gain useful insights into the topics under review. Do not hesitate to ask questions beyond those appearing in the study guide—remember that the guide is merely a tool to help you take advantage of valuable ideas and strategies for moving beyond the hurt of mistreatment.*

6. *Close in prayer, thanking God for his love and care and asking him to help you apply his wisdom to your own situation.*

Study Guide

Chapter One: The First Step

A. Mistreatment is one of the painful common denominators of human experience. We all know what it means to be unfairly treated in some arena of our lives—in childhood, in marriage, in our friendships, at school, at church, on the job, and even by society in the form of crime, discrimination, or other kinds of injustice. When abused by a family member, misjudged by a boss, or betrayed by a friend, our first response is, "I don't deserve this! It's not fair!" [Page 12]

> *Dear friends, do not be surprised at the painful trial you are suffering, as though something strange were happening to you. But rejoice that you participate in the sufferings of Christ, so that you may be overjoyed when his glory is revealed. . . . So then, those who suffer according to God's will should commit themselves to their faithful Creator and continue to do good.*

> 1 Peter 4:12-13, 19

> *They preached the good news in that city and won a large number of disciples. Then they returned to Lystra, Iconium and Antioch, strengthening the disciples and encouraging them to remain true to the faith. "We must go through many hardships to enter the kingdom of God," they said.*

> Acts 14:21-22

Discussion Questions

1. What is your first reaction to these statements about the inevitability of suffering or hardship? How do they make you feel?

2. How does the 1 Peter passage instruct us to think about suffering? How does it say we are *not* to react? Why are these things difficult? Why does the passage say we should "rejoice"?

3. In Acts 14:21-22, Paul and his companions are trying to "encourage" and "strengthen" young believers. Why, then, do you think they warned these believers about undergoing hardships? How encouraging could this be? What do you suppose was Paul's motive?

4. How do these verses apply to mistreatment in your own life? Which part of these verses is hardest for you to take? Why?

B.   I don't pretend that these strategies are foolproof "handles" for solving your problems, nor am I claiming that the road to emotional freedom will be an easy one. You will need courage, commitment, and honesty along the way. All things worth achieving require serious work, and the achievement of emotional wholeness is no exception. [Pages 13-14]

All hard work brings a profit, but mere talk leads only to poverty.

Proverbs 14:23

Therefore, my dear friends, as you have always obeyed—not only in my presence, but now much more in my absence— continue to work out your salvation with fear and trembling, for it is God who works in you to will and to act according to his good purpose.

Philippians 2:12-13

Discussion Questions

1. Of the three qualities needed to gain emotional wholeness—courage, commitment, and honesty— which is the most difficult for you? Why? What can you do to help overcome this obstacle?

2. What does Proverbs 14:23 suggest about your own "road to emotional freedom"? How, specifically, can you move toward the first half of the verse and away from the second?

3. In Philippians 2:12-13, Paul does not mean that we work *to gain* or *to earn* our salvation; rather, he means that we cooperate with God in making our salvation evident to everyone. God worked our salvation *in*; we work it *out*. How might this idea relate to your trial of mistreatment?

4. How does the knowledge that emotional wholeness comes only with hard work and effort help to smooth out the road to recovery? How might ignoring these facts hinder the healing process?

Chapter Two: A Quantum Leap

A. The bitterness that follows mistreatment often threatens to control us. Our memories are acid-etched with anger, resentment, self-pity. Hate boils in us, filling us with the desire for revenge. Anger turns inward and becomes depression. We know we should forgive. Sometimes we want to forgive. But those bitter feelings keep coming back and we have no control over them. [Page 21]

> *Make every effort to live in peace with all men and to be holy; without holiness no one will see the Lord. See to it that no one misses the grace of God and that no bitter root grows up to cause trouble and defile many.*

Hebrews 12:14-15

> *Do not repay evil with evil or insult with insult, but with blessing, because to this you were called so that you may inherit a blessing. For,*
>
> *"Whoever would love life*
> *and see good days*
> *must keep his tongue from evil*
> *and his lips from deceitful speech.*
> *He must turn from evil and do good;*
> *he must seek peace and pursue it.*
> *For the eyes of the Lord are on the righteous*
> *and his ears are attentive to their prayer,*
> *but the face of the Lord is against*
> *those who do evil."*

1 Peter 3:9-12

Discussion Questions

1. Think about someone you know who is controlled by bitterness. How would you describe this person? Is he or she pleasant to be around? What does this bitterness do to his or her relationships? Does this bitterness accomplish anything constructive?

2. What is the connection in Hebrews 12:14-15 between being "holy" and being "bitter"? What metaphor does the writer use to describe bitterness? Does this suggest anything about the way to get rid of it?

3. What does 1 Peter 3:9-12 say we must avoid? What does it say we are to do? What benefit is promised? Why is it important to remember these things when we are mistreated?

4. Both biblical passages declare that Christians should try to "live in peace" or "seek peace and pursue it." What might this mean in your situation? If you are not currently in a strained relationship, how would you encourage a fellow Christian to follow these instructions?

B. The self-destructive power of bitterness was vividly described by Harry Emerson Fosdick when he said, "Resentment is where you burn down your own house to kill a rat." [Page 22]

Resentment kills a fool,
and envy slays the simple.

Job 5:2

The entire law is summed up in a single command: "Love your neighbor as yourself." If you keep on biting and devouring each other, watch out or you will be destroyed by each other.

Galatians 5:14-15

Discussion Questions

1. In your own words, describe what Fosdick meant about resentment. Do you agree with him? Why or why not?

2. How does resentment "kill" or envy "slay"? Whom do they destroy? How can you tell if someone fits these categories?

3. Paul gives two reasons in Galatians 5:14-15 for restraining ourselves when we are tempted to act out our bitterness. What are they?

4. Remember that these verses were written to *believers*. Why is that fact significant? What do these verses say to *you*?

C. The key to emotional wholeness is a new perspective, a new attitude, a new way of looking at life. By God's grace, we can choose a perspective on mistreatment that says, "Whatever happens to me, I expect God to transform it into something good." [Page 27]

God causes all things to work together for good to those who love God, to those who are called according to His purpose.

Romans 8:28 (NASB)

*Now I want you to know, brothers, that
what has happened to me has really served
to advance the gospel. As a result, it has
become clear throughout the whole palace
guard and to everyone else that I am in
chains for Christ. Because of my chains,
most of the brothers in the Lord have been
encouraged to speak the word of God more
courageously and fearlessly. It is true that
some preach Christ out of envy and rivalry,
but others out of good will. The latter do so
in love, knowing that I am put here for the
defense of the gospel. The former preach
Christ out of selfish ambition, not sincerely,
supposing that they can stir up trouble for
me while I am in chains. But what does it
matter? The important thing is that in every
way, whether from false motives or true,
Christ is preached. And because of this I
rejoice.*

Philippians 1:12-18a

Discussion Questions

1. How is this advice about adopting a new perspective different from wishful thinking? How is it unlike
looking at the world "through rose-colored glasses"?

2. Note that Romans 8:28 says all things "work
together for good. . . ." How does this differ from
saying "all things work for good"? What might this
imply about the length of time required for this good
to become evident?

3. Describe Paul's circumstances as pictured in
Philippians (see especially 1:7, 17, 30, 4:11-14). What

hardship was he undergoing? Did he deserve such treatment? Why or why not? What shifts in perspective did he make? How can he be an example for us?

4. What possible new perspective can you bring to your trial of mistreatment? How could this perspective help you not only to cope with your situation, but to thrive in it?

D. The new perspective on mistreatment which leads to emotional wholeness says, "I understand that injustice and mistreatment are a part of life. I can't always control what others do to me, but I can control how I will respond to them. I choose to forgive. I choose to get on with my life. I trust the fact that God can take all the circumstances of my life, even the painful circumstances of mistreatment, and weave them together in a pattern that brings about good in my own life and in the lives of others around me." [Pages 27-28]

> *I have told you these things, so that in me you may have peace. In this world you will have trouble. But take heart! I have overcome the world.*

John 16:33

> *Therefore I will boast all the more gladly about my weaknesses, so that Christ's power may rest on me. That is why, for Christ's sake, I delight in weaknesses, in insults, in hardships, in persecutions, in difficulties. For when I am weak, then I am strong.*

2 Corinthians 12:9b-10

Discussion Questions

1. Divide the highlighted paragraph from *Mistreated* into a series of single statements—for example, "1. Injustice is a part of life; 2. I can't control what others do," etc. Which of these statements makes the biggest impression on you? Why?

2. How do Jesus' words in John 16:33 present a new perspective to his disciples? How could this perspective have helped them cope during the ordeal they were about to suffer?

3. In 2 Corinthians 12, Paul saw the difficult and painful circumstances of his life as opportunities for something wonderful to happen to him. What was it? How did his new perspective help him through his ordeal with the "thorn in [the] flesh" mentioned in 12:7? Is such a perspective possible for you? If so, how? If not, why not?

4. How might God be able to take *your* pain and weave it into "a pattern that brings about good" in your life and in the lives of others? What can you do to get started in that direction?

Chapter Three: You Are Not a Victim

A. Lauren, Scott, and Janet are good, caring, conscientious people who have tried to live upright lives. In return, they have been betrayed or slandered or used and tossed aside. They have been cast in the role of victims and unless they find a way to escape that role, the hurt that was done to them once in their lives will continue to hurt them again and again. [Page 33]

We are hard pressed on every side, but not crushed; perplexed, but not in despair; persecuted, but not abandoned; struck down, but not destroyed.

2 Corinthians 4:8-9

Discussion Questions

1. Have you ever been hurt like Janet, Scott, or Lauren? Did you feel like a victim? How could such a "victim mentality" continue to hurt you again and again?

2. How do Paul's words in 2 Corinthians 4:8-9 show he has not succumbed to a victim mentality? What is the one, overarching impression you get of Paul from this passage?

3. Where did Paul get this kind of strength? What did it enable him to do? Did it solve all his problems? How can you tap this same source of strength? (see 4:5-7)

4. Write out a paragraph stating what you will do in order to get out of or stay out of a victim mentality. If you are doing this study with others, read your paragraph out loud and get reactions from the group. Pray with each other for God's strength.

B. As long as we harbor bitterness toward the person who has hurt us, we allow that person to control and victimize us. We may be carrying the memories of some mistreatment that happened ten, twenty, or thirty years ago, and the person who hurt us may even be dead and buried—but as long as we clutch the bitterness of that mistreatment, we continue to be negatively, emotionally bound to those who hurt us. They continue to pull our strings and push our buttons, to control our emotions and our responses—but only if we let them. [Page 35]

> *Get rid of all bitterness, rage and anger,*
> *brawling and slander, along with every*
> *form of malice. Be kind and compassion-*
> *ate to one another, forgiving each other,*
> *just as in Christ God forgave you.*
>
> Ephesians 4:31-32

Read 2 Samuel 3:20-30; 1 Kings 2:13-34.

Discussion Questions

1. When we refuse to let go of bitterness toward someone, how does that person still "control" or "victimize" us? Have you ever experienced this? Briefly describe the situation.

2. According to Ephesians 4:31-32, why should we "get rid of all bitterness . . . forgiving each other"? Is it possible to "be kind and compassionate" to those who have maliciously hurt us? If so, how?

3. The story of Joab, King David's general, is told in 2 Samuel 3:20-30 and 1 Kings 2:13-34. Joab had a problem with bitterness that ultimately destroyed him. What caused his bitterness? How did it finally ruin him? What can we learn from his life?

4. Not all bitterness is immediately recognizable, but there are frequently signs that accompany it. What signs can you identify that point to bitterness? Do

any of these signs mark your life? If so, what action do you need to take?

C. Again and again, I've gone back to a little booklet called *Seven Secrets to Spiritual Power*, written by A. W. Tozer. One of Tozer's seven secrets is this: "Never defend yourself." Yes, we defend people who have no one else to defend them. Yes, we do what we can to clarify communication, to correct misunderstandings. But we will never move out of the victim role until we stop being defensive. [Page 39]

> *Nebuchadnezzar said to them, "Is it true, Shadrach, Meshach and Abednego, that you do not serve my gods or worship the image of gold I have set up? Now when you hear the sound of the horn, flute, zither, lyre, harp, pipes and all kinds of music, if you are ready to fall down and worship the image I made, very good. But if you do not worship it, you will be thrown immediately into a blazing furnace. Then what god will be able to rescue you from my hand?" Shadrach, Meshach and Abednego replied to the king, "O Nebuchadnezzar, we do not need to defend ourselves before you in this matter. If we are thrown into the blazing furnace, the God we serve is able to save us from it, and he will rescue us from your hand, O king. But even if he does not, we want you to know, O king, that we will not serve your gods or worship the image of gold you have set up."*

> Daniel 3:14-18

When words are many, sin is not absent,
but he who holds his tongue is wise.

Proverbs 10:19

Discussion Questions

1. How does defending yourself tend to keep you in a victim role?

2. The three young Hebrews in Daniel 3 gave several theological reasons why they refused to defend themselves. What were some of those reasons? Are they valid today? Why or why not?

3. We are most apt to defend ourselves when we are emotionally upset. How can the wisdom of Proverbs 10:19 help us when we find ourselves in those kinds of situations?

4. In what circumstances are you most likely to try defending yourself? What has happened in the past when you have done so? How can you improve in this area?

D. Prisoners were shot, beaten, burned, hacked by machetes, asphyxiated, emasculated, bayoneted, and subjected to biological experiments. Yet, even as the ferocity of the prison officials intensified, the will and resistance of the prisoners grew stronger. Valladares and his fellow prisoners engaged in peaceful protests, hunger strikes, work stoppages. When the political commissioner of the prison asked Valladares where the prisoners got the strength to go on in the face of hunger and torture, he replied, "We have an inexhaustible supply of strength, sir, an imperishable source called love." [Page 45]

If you love those who love you, what credit is that to you? Even 'sinners' love those who love them. And if you do good to those who are good to you, what credit is that to you? Even 'sinners' do that. . . . But love your enemies, do good to them, and lend to them without expecting to get anything back. Then your reward will be great, and you will be sons of the Most High, because he is kind to the ungrateful and wicked.

Luke 6:32-33, 35

Discussion Questions

1. If you had been the political commissioner at Isla de Piños, how might you have expected Valladares to answer your question? If you had been in Valladares's place, what might you have replied? What is your reaction to Valladares's words?

2. In what ways did Jesus act on his own instructions in Luke 6:32-33? In what ways did his disciples? In what ways do you?

3. What is the result of loving your enemies (v. 35)? What is the connection between being "sons of the Most High" and the fact that God "is kind to the ungrateful and wicked"?

4. Who are your enemies? List them. What *specifically* can you do for them in line with Luke 6:32-35?

Chapter Four: The 50:20 Principle

A. When we are mistreated, it is only natural that we want to fight back, to get even. That's a basic instinct in the human species. But God wants us to move beyond mere animal response. The image of God was stamped upon us at creation, was broken by sin, and is now being restored in us as God seeks to conform us (as Romans 8:28-29 tells us) into the image of Christ. And the image God has given us in the example of his Son Jesus is an image of forgiveness and mercy, not revenge. [Page 54]

Do not repay anyone evil for evil. Be careful to do what is right in the eyes of everybody. If it is possible, as far as it depends on you, live at peace with everyone. Do not take revenge, my friends, but leave room for God's wrath, for it is written: "It is mine to avenge; I will repay," says the Lord. On the contrary:

"If your enemy is hungry, feed him;
if he is thirsty, give him something
*   to drink.*
In doing this, you will heap burning
*   coals on his head."*
Do not be overcome by evil, but
*   overcome evil with good.*

Romans 12:17-21

Discussion Questions

1. Is desire for revenge ever a problem for you? In what circumstances?

2. What reason does Romans 12:19 give for not

taking revenge? Why is this the best option?

3. What action does Paul suggest we take in Romans 12:20? What examples of this can you describe from your own experience?

4. What does Romans 12:21 mean to you? How can you ensure that both halves of this verse are equally true of your life?

B.   Joseph would have affirmed the words of Frederick Buechner, "To lick your wounds, to smack your lips over grievances long past, to roll over your tongue the prospect of bitter confrontations still to come, to savor to the last toothsome morsel both the pain you are given and the pain you are giving back—in many ways it is a feast fit for a king. The chief drawback is that what you are wolfing down is yourself. The skeleton at the feast is you." [Page 55]

He who digs a hole and scoops it out
falls into the pit he has made.
The trouble he causes recoils on himself;
his violence comes down on his own head.

Psalm 7:15-16

Discussion Questions

1. What seems pleasant to us about rehearsing old hurts and savoring "to the last toothsome morsel both the pain you are given and the pain you are giving back"? What does such behavior leave with us in the end?

2. Do you see Psalm 7:15-16 as a promise or a warning? Why?

3. What biblical examples can you name where bitterness or revenge ended in tragedy for all involved? What examples can you cite from your own experience?

4. Meditate on Psalm 7:15-16, then rewrite it in your own words. Take this version and put it for two weeks in a location where you will see it often. Ask God to remind you of the dangers of harboring bitterness.

C. What a temptation it would be to possess absolute power over the person who once mistreated you! Joseph had that kind of absolute power. If you had been in Joseph's place, how would you have handled his power? [Page 56]

> *When Joseph's brothers saw that their father was dead, they said, "What if Joseph holds a grudge against us and pays us back for all the wrongs we did to him?" So they sent word to Joseph, saying, "Your father left these instructions before he died: 'This is what you are to say to Joseph: I ask you to forgive your brothers the sins and the wrongs they committed in treating you so badly.' Now please forgive the sins of the servants of the God of your father." When their message came to him, Joseph wept. His brothers then came and threw themselves down before him. "We are your slaves," they said. But Joseph said to them, "Don't be afraid. Am I in the place of God? You intended to harm me, but God intended it for good to accomplish what is now being*

done, the saving of many lives. So then, don't be afraid. I will provide for you and your children." And he reassured them and spoke kindly to them.

Genesis 50:15-21

[Jesus] sent messengers on ahead, who went into a Samaritan village to get things ready for him; but the people there did not welcome him, because he was heading for Jerusalem. When the disciples James and John saw this, they asked, "Lord, do you want us to call fire down from heaven to destroy them?" But Jesus turned and rebuked them.

Luke 9:52-55

Discussion Questions

1. Respond to Ron's question: If you had been in Joseph's place, how would you have handled his power?

2. What did Joseph mean when he said, "Am I in the place of God"? On what basis did Joseph exhort his brothers to be unafraid?

3. What motives do you think prompted the question of James and John in Luke 9:54? What motivated Jesus to answer as he did?

4. Paul reminds us in 1 Corinthians 6:2-3 that our behavior should be consistent with the awesome position we will one day hold. If you had to rate yourself on a scale of 1 (poor) to 10 (excellent) on

your present-day use of power, what score would you earn? Explain.

D. A little girl was once asked to define the word forgiveness. She thought a moment, then said, "I think it's like the pretty smell a flower makes when somebody steps on it." [Page 59]

Be kind and compassionate to one another, forgiving each other, just as in Christ God forgave you. Be imitators of God, therefore, as dearly loved children and live a life of love, just as Christ loved us and gave himself up for us as a fragrant offering and sacrifice to God.

Ephesians 4:32-5:2

Discussion Questions

1. The little girl's definition of forgiveness makes us smile. What other word pictures of forgiveness can you create? What is forgiveness like to you?

2. How is the little girl's "pretty smell a flower makes when somebody steps on it" like Jesus' "fragrant offering and sacrifice to God"?

3. Ephesians 4:32-5:1 says Christians are forgiven by God and are therefore "dearly loved children." If these two things were not true, what would be your situation? What is required of you if they are true?

4. Listed below are five qualities that Ephesians 4:32-5:2 says should characterize every Christian. Beside each quality, name one thing you can do to demonstrate that quality to someone who has mistreated you.

kind _____

compassionate _____

forgiving _____

imitator of God _____

live a life of love _____

Chapter Five: The Freedom of Forgiveness

A. Whenever two sides of a conflict are willing to commit themselves to the hard work of rebuilding trust and understanding, then a broken marriage, a damaged parent-child relationship, or a church division can be healed. In fact, the commitment and unconditional love of just one side of a conflict is often enough to melt the resistance of the other party and so bring about reconciliation. [Page 66]

I plead with Euodia and I plead with Syntyche to agree with each other in the Lord. Yes, and I ask you, loyal yokefellow, help these women who have contended at my side in the cause of the gospel, along with Clement and the rest of my fellow workers, whose names are in the book of life.

Philippians 4:2-3

God . . . reconciled us to himself through Christ and gave us the ministry of reconciliation.

2 Corinthians 5:18

Discussion Questions

1. Do you agree with the statement, "Whenever two sides of a conflict are willing to commit themselves to the hard work of rebuilding trust and understanding . . . [that relationship] can be healed"? Explain.

2. On what basis does Paul plead with his two friends to reconcile? Are they asked to do this alone? How might this be important?

3. According to 2 Corinthians 5:18, what role have believers been given by God? How do you fit into this ministry?

4. During times of mistreatment, do you identify more with the person who shows "commitment and unconditional love" or with the "resistant other party"? Are you satisfied with that status? Explain.

B. Our emotional well-being does not depend upon what others do or fail to do toward us. Even when the offender chooses to leave the relationship broken, you and I can still be whole people. Forgiveness is unilateral, it is something we do all alone, right in our own hearts. Reconciliation depends on two people coming together, but forgiveness only depends on you. [Page 67]

> *Then Peter came to Jesus and asked, "Lord, how many times shall I forgive my brother when he sins against me? Up to seven times?" Jesus answered, "I tell you, not seven times, but seventy times seven times."*

Matthew 18:21-22 (NIV, margin)

Father, forgive them, for they do not know what they are doing.

Luke 23:34

While they were stoning him, Stephen prayed, "Lord Jesus, receive my spirit." Then he fell on his knees and cried out, "Lord, do not hold this sin against them."

Acts 7:59-60a

Discussion Questions

1. Describe the difference between forgiveness and reconciliation. When does this difference become important?

2. What attitude does Jesus require of us in Matthew 18:21-22? What makes this demand difficult to accomplish? What makes it possible?

3. How are the words of Jesus in Luke 23:34 and those of Stephen in Acts 7:60 alike? How does mistreatment give us an opportunity to follow their examples?

4. Is there anyone in your life whom you have as yet refused to forgive? If so, name the person. Then read Luke 23:26-34 and Acts 7:54-60, afterwards asking God to give you the desire to follow the example of Stephen and Jesus.

C. The person who remains in bitterness eventually begins to direct that bitterness toward God. What that person is really saying is, "All these experiences in my life added up to evil. How could

God allow so much evil and mistreatment in my life?" The only healthy and realistic response is to realize that it's the painful things in life that God uses to build our character. [Page 72]

> *Endure hardship as discipline; God is treating you as sons. For what son is not disciplined by his father? If you are not disciplined (and everyone undergoes discipline), then you are illegitimate children and not true sons. Moreover, we have all had human fathers who disciplined us and we respected them for it. How much more should we submit to the Father of our spirits and live! Our fathers disciplined us for a little while as they thought best; but God disciplines us for our good, that we may share in his holiness. No discipline seems pleasant at the time, but painful. Later on, however, it produces a harvest of righteousness and peace for those who have been trained by it.*

Hebrews 12:7-11

Discussion Questions

1. What is it about us that makes it necessary for God to use painful things in life to build our character? Wouldn't pleasant things work just as well?

2. The writer of Hebrews asks us to make a perspective shift when he writes, "Endure hardship as discipline; God is treating you as sons." What shift is he asking us to make? How would it help us in times of trouble or mistreatment?

3. According to Hebrews 12:10, what is God's purpose in allowing hardship into our lives? What comparison does the writer make between God's discipline and that of our human fathers?

4. According to verse 11, is discipline pleasant at the time we go through it? What is it supposed to produce in us? When does it produce these things? For whom does it produce them? Do you fit into this category? Why or why not?

Chapter Six: The Healing of Memories

A. For anyone who has endured the hurt of mistreatment, healing of memories is a crucial issue. Many of us desperately need to grow and change beyond our painful memories, to release the past and its pain, and to get on with our lives. [Page 82]

> *For I am the least of the apostles and do not even deserve to be called an apostle, because I persecuted the church of God. But by the grace of God I am what I am, and his grace to me was not without effect.*

> 1 Corinthians 15:9-10a

> *Although I am less than the least of all God's people, this grace was given me: to preach to the Gentiles the unsearchable riches of Christ.*

> Ephesians 3:8

> *Even though I was once a blasphemer and a persecutor and a violent man, I was*

*shown mercy because I acted in ignorance
and unbelief. The grace of our Lord was
poured out on me abundantly, along with
the faith and love that are in Christ Jesus.
Here is a trustworthy saying that deserves
full acceptance: Christ Jesus came into the
world to save sinners—of whom I am the
worst.*

1 Timothy 1:13-15

Discussion Questions

1. How can painful memories chain you to the past
and thus prevent you from getting on with your life?
Do you know someone who is "stuck in the past"
because of past mistreatment? Describe his or her
situation.

2. What was the painful memory that Paul recalled in
the three passages above? Who was the offender?
How could this memory have affected the apostle's
ministry?

3. Paul obviously did not "forget" this painful
memory, but he did move beyond it. How? To what
did he attribute his ability to get beyond the pain of
his past?

4. What clues in these passages would help you
move beyond the pain of your past? How can it help
to remember that the great apostle struggled with
similar issues?

B. Healing of memories has to take place at the
experiential and feelings level. It has to reorder our

perspective and change our feelings associated with the mistreatment. We don't need to have our intellects walked through a visualization process. It is our emotions which need to experience a memorable event fragrant with the healing presence of Christ. [Page 92]

> *The Lord is my shepherd, I shall not*
>   *be in want.*
>   *He makes me lie down in green pastures,*
> *he leads me beside quiet waters,*
>   *he restores my soul.*
> *He guides me in paths of righteousness*
>   *for his name's sake.*
> *Even though I walk*
>   *through the valley of the shadow of death,*
> *I will fear no evil,*
>   *for you are with me;*
> *your rod and your staff,*
>   *they comfort me.*
> *You prepare a table before me*
>   *in the presence of my enemies.*
> *You anoint my head with oil;*
>   *my cup overflows.*
> *Surely goodness and love will follow me*
>   *all the days of my life,*
> *and I will dwell in the house of the* Lord
>   *forever.*

Psalm 23

Discussion Questions

1. Why don't our intellects need to be "walked through a visualization process"? Why can't there be

complete healing merely through the acceptance of certain facts?

2. What pictures come to mind as you read Psalm 23? What effect do these pictures have on you? When you think of Jesus as the "good shepherd" (see John 10:14), what images do you "see"?

3. Scripture is full of powerful pictures: the godly like trees planted by a stream (Psalm 1:3), God like a mother comforting her child (Isaiah 66:13), the church like a beautiful bride (Revelation 21:2), evangelism like a farmer sowing seed (Mark 4:3-8). What Scriptural pictures speak most strongly to your hurt or pain? How can you use these pictures to speed the healing process?

4. The last line of Psalm 23 says, "Surely goodness and love will follow me all the days of my life, and I will dwell in the house of the LORD forever." Meditate on this for several minutes. What does it mean for you?

C. Clara Barton, the founder of the American Red Cross, had a well-known reputation as someone who never held a grudge. Once, when a friend reminded her of a wrong done to her some years earlier, she seemed not to know what her friend was talking about. "Surely you must remember!" said the friend.

"No," Clara replied without hesitation. "I distinctly remember forgetting that." [Page 94]

Bear with each other and forgive whatever grievances you may have against one another. Forgive as the Lord forgave you.

Colossians 3:13

[The Lord said through Jeremiah,] For I will forgive their wickedness and will remember their sins no more.

Hebrews 8:12

Discussion Questions

1. How can someone "remember" to "forget"? What was Clara Barton saying?

2. Paul says Christians must "bear with each other." Why is that necessary? What does it imply? What kind of grievances are we to forgive? On what basis do we forgive?

3. In what way is the Lord's statement in Hebrews 8:12 an example for us? In what way is it unique to him?

4. How is "forgiving" and "forgetting" important to your own well-being? What strategy do you use to achieve this?

Chapter Seven: Courage to Confront

A. Sometimes love must be tough, sometimes love must confront. It is not always genuinely loving to be "tolerant" and "longsuffering" when someone mistreats us. It may simply be that we wish to avoid the unpleasant emotions of confrontation. Or we may lack assertiveness. Or we may be afraid. The result of such timidity or indifference can lead to tragedy. [Page 96]

> *Better is open rebuke*
> *than hidden love.*
> *Wounds from a friend can be trusted,*
> *but an enemy multiplies kisses.*

Proverbs 27:5, 6

> *Let a righteous man strike me—it is a*
> *kindness;*
> *let him rebuke me—it is oil on my head.*
> *My head will not refuse it.*

Psalm 141:5

Discussion Questions

1. Do you sometimes overlook an offense rather than confront the offender? Why? Has this ever made the situation worse? If so, how?

2. Why is "open rebuke" better than "hidden love"? How can "wounds" ever be better than "kisses"?

3. What kind of person does the psalmist invite to "strike" him? What does this say about the kind of character we need in order to confront effectively?

4. Think of the times someone has confronted you. Then take a sheet of paper and divide it in two. On one side, write down the ineffective or offensive ways you have been confronted. On the other side, list the effective or thoughtful ways someone has confronted you. Use these lists as helpful guides the next time you are called to confront wrong behavior.

B. If we say we love someone, how can we allow him or her to continue in destructive behavior?

If we are afraid to speak the truth, how can we claim to genuinely love? If we blithely allow someone to continue in behavior that is destructive, abusive, unethical, or immoral, then we are not acting in love. We are actually enabling and contributing to the brokenness of that person. Such behavior—which we try to pass off as "tolerance"—is worse than hatred. For it is really indifference, the true opposite of love. [Page 97]

> *If your brother sins against you, go and show him his fault, just between the two of you. If he listens to you, you have won your brother over.*

Matthew 18:15

> *Carry each other's burdens, and in this way you will fulfill the law of Christ.*

Galatians 6:2

Discussion Questions

1. In what way can it be said that indifference, not hate, is the "true opposite of love"?

2. How does Jesus tell us to confront a brother in Matthew 18:15? In what way(s) do we sometimes ignore this command? What is the purpose of this confrontation?

3. How do we "fulfill the law of Christ" according to Galatians 6:2? What does this mean? How does this relate to confrontation?

4. As odd as it may sound, confrontation is really about love. Take a few minutes to define for yourself the term "loving confrontation." What does it

involve? How is it done? What is its goal? Who is its focus?

C. Before confronting, we look first to our own hearts: Are we confronting out of genuine love for the offender or because we can't wait to set him or her straight? Do we choose words that heal or words that hammer home our point? Do we approach the offender in loving sorrow over the broken relationship or do we attack him in anger? Do we genuinely want to rebuild the relationship or do we just want to get something off our chests? [Page 105]

> *Brothers, if someone is caught in a sin, you who are spiritual should restore him gently. But watch yourself, or you also may be tempted.*

Galatians 6:1

> *. . . speaking the truth in love, we will in all things grow up into him who is the Head, that is, Christ.*

Ephesians 4:15

Discussion Questions

1. Read again the paragraph from *Mistreated* quoted above. Which of those styles of confrontation is normally your first impulse? If this first impulse is bad, how can you overcome it?

2. What attitudes does Paul in Galatians 6:1 require of those who would confront sin? Why does he say these attitudes are important?

3. What is the goal of all Christian communication—including confrontation—according to Ephesians 4:15? How can loving confrontation help move us in this direction? How can unloving confrontation move us away from it?

4. The next time you find yourself having to confront someone, first spend twenty minutes reading through the "Love Chapter" of 1 Corinthians 13. Insert your name wherever the word "love" appears. Then ask God to help you be an example of love to the one you must confront.

Chapter Eight: The Power of Positive People

A.   Edison was unstoppable because he never gave up on the future. He never stopped working, never stopped risking. [Page 113]

> *We do not want you to be uninformed, brothers, about the hardships we suffered in the province of Asia. We were under great pressure, far beyond our ability to endure, so that we despaired even of life. Indeed, in our hearts we felt the sentence of death. But this happened that we might not rely on ourselves but on God, who raises the dead. He has delivered us from such a deadly peril, and he will deliver us. On him we have set our hope that he will continue to deliver us.*

2 Corinthians 1:8-10

Discussion Questions

1. Would you have liked to work with Thomas Edison? Why?

2. What do you think was Paul's purpose in telling his Corinthian friends about his troubles in the province of Asia? Why did he not want them to be "uninformed"?

3. Where did Paul get his confidence? On what was his hope set? How is that same cause for confidence available to you?

4. Think of ten specific ways you can be a source of optimism to one person who is close to you. Get out a calendar and plan how and when you will "spring" these things on that person in the next month.

B.   There's an old adage that an optimist sees an opportunity in every calamity, while a pessimist sees a calamity in every opportunity. What is your perspective on your trial of mistreatment? Does it look like a calamity or an opportunity? Your answer to that question will have a profound effect on your ability to reshape your future and move beyond mistreatment. [Page 117]

> *Therefore we do not lose heart. Though outwardly we are wasting away, yet inwardly we are being renewed day by day. For our light and momentary troubles are achieving for us an eternal glory that far outweighs them all. So we fix our eyes not on what is seen, but on what is unseen. For what is seen is temporary, but what is unseen is eternal.*
>
> 2 Corinthians 4:16-18

Discussion Questions

1. Answer Ron's question: Does your trial of mistreatment look to you like a calamity or an opportunity? Why?

2. Why did Paul not "lose heart"? To what did he look forward? How does the text show that you, too, can tap into this attitude?

3. Where did Paul fix his gaze when things got tough? How is this helpful?

4. Find five Scripture passages (other than this one) that talk about being committed to a long-range vision, to an "ultimate outlook." Discuss what you find with other Christian friends.

C.   Ultimately, the issue of mistreatment forces us to face this question: Do we believe God is in control? Do we believe he either wills or allows everything that happens in our lives? If we really believe that, we become unstoppable, because we refuse to let past disappointments shape our future. Because we believe God is in control and that he is unlimited, we believe the future is limitless as well. Regardless of how the past has hurt us, we know who holds the future, and we are excited and optimistic about tomorrow. [Page 118]

> *Who can speak and have it happen if the Lord has not decreed it? Is it not from the mouth of the Most High that both calamities and good things come?*

Lamentations 3:37-38

Are not two sparrows sold for a penny? Yet not one of them will fall to the ground apart from the will of your Father. And even the very hairs of your head are all numbered. So don't be afraid; you are worth more than many sparrows.

Matthew 10:29-31

Discussion Questions

1. How can a belief in the sovereignty of God encourage a positive outlook on life? Why do you think many people resist the idea of a sovereign God?

2. Does the passage from Lamentations encourage you or discourage you? Why? How did this idea affect the prophet Jeremiah, who wrote it?

3. What point is Jesus trying to make in Matthew 10:29-31? How does this point relate to your own mistreatment?

4. There are two ways people often think of the sovereignty of God. One says, "Since God is sovereign and he is good, I know things will eventually work out for the best." The other says, "Since God is in control and he has allowed pain to come into my life, he must be bad." How would you help someone decide which viewpoint was true?

D. I believe God is calling you and me to a kind of "godly optimism" which is rooted in a realistic understanding of the evils of this world, which understands that the systems and dynamics of our culture are under satanic domination, which acknowledges that injustice and mistreatment are to be expected in this life—yet which does not despair, give up, or become embittered. How, in the face of all the world's evil, can we keep an optimistic outlook? Because Jesus is the King, God is the Judge, and all that is now wrong will one day be made right. One day, all wounds will be healed, all tears will be wiped away, all sorrow will be no more. [Page 121]

> *Now we know that if the earthly tent we live in is destroyed, we have a building from God, an eternal house in heaven, not built by human hands. Meanwhile we groan, longing to be clothed with our heavenly dwelling, because when we are clothed, we will not be found naked. For while we are in this tent, we groan and are burdened, because we do not wish to be unclothed but to be clothed with our heavenly dwelling, so that what is mortal may be swallowed up by life. Now it is God who has made us for this very purpose and has given us the Spirit as a deposit, guaranteeing what is to come. Therefore we are always confident . . .*

2 Corinthians 5:1-6a

Discussion Questions

1. Does looking at the world's sin and evil challenge you or depress you? How is it possible to be optimistic in a deteriorating culture?

2. Did Paul, in 2 Corinthians 5:1-6, deny that he was experiencing hard times? Did he say we shouldn't

talk about it? What was his attitude toward hardship?

3. How can we be sure that we will triumph in the end? What bearing does this assurance have on our present activities?

4. Would you say that you are a natural pessimist or an optimist? Do you like being around optimists or pessimists? Why?

Chapter Nine: Somebody's Watching You

A. What will you do with today and tomorrow? How will you shape the time that is in your hands? Will you break the cycle of mistreatment or will you pass on your hurt to others? Will you continue in the old, failed patterns of the past or are you ready to build a new life for yourself, a life free of bitterness and resentment? And what are you teaching your children and the others around you who are watching your life? What are you teaching them by your response to mistreatment? [Pages 133-134]

> *Amon was twenty-two years old when he became king, and he reigned in Jerusalem two years. His mother's name was Meshullemeth daughter of Haruz; she was from Jotbah. He did evil in the eyes of the LORD, as his father Manasseh had done. He walked in all the ways of his father; he worshiped the idols his father had worshiped, and bowed down to them. He forsook the LORD, the God of his fathers, and did not walk in the way of the LORD.*
>
> 2 Kings 21:19-22 (See also 2 Kings 23:31-32, 36-37; 24:8-9, 18-19.)

I have set before you life and death, blessings and curses. Now choose life, so that you and your children may live.

Deuteronomy 30:19

Discussion Questions

1. Answer Ron's question: What are you teaching others by your response to mistreatment?

2. Does the phrase "He walked in all the ways of his father" hearten you or chill you? Why?

3. Deuteronomy 30:19 was spoken to ancient Israel right before the nation entered the Promised Land, but the words have meaning for all believers everywhere. What choice is given? Whom does the choice affect? How will you choose?

4. Take a chance and ask someone close to you what he or she learns from *watching* you, not necessarily from *listening* to you. What did you learn?

B. You and I have an enormous responsibility that is far too easy to pass off lightly. Our neighbors, our co-workers, our friends, our family, and most of all our children are watching us, observing how we function under fire. Whether you like it or not, you are living out your life in a fishbowl. Somebody is watching you. What is that person learning from you about a godly, therapeutic response to mistreatment? [Page 135]

You are the light of the world. A city on a hill cannot be hidden. Neither do people

*light a lamp and put it under a bowl.
Instead they put it on its stand, and it gives
light to everyone in the house. In the same
way, let your light shine before men, that
they may see your good deeds and praise
your Father in heaven.*

Matthew 5:14-16

*Watch your life and doctrine closely.
Persevere in them, because if you do, you
will save both yourself and your hearers.*

1 Timothy 4:16

Discussion Questions

1. Who is watching *you* "in the fishbowl"? Name them. What lessons may they already have learned from you about "a godly, therapeutic response to mistreatment"?

2. What sort of "light" is streaming from you? Notice that Jesus says we are to "*let* your light shine before men. . . ." That implies a choice must be made. What choice are you making?

3. What does Paul tell Timothy to watch in 1 Timothy 4:16? What else is he to do with these things? Why?

4. In your trial of mistreatment, in what areas are you most likely to "shine"? In what areas do you need help? Identify these strengths and weaknesses and ask God to help you "give light to everyone in the house."

C. The small choices you and I make, whether for good or ill, become enormously magnified in the lives of those around us. Whenever you suffer mistreatment, you are given the opportunity to influence others by the example of your response. We don't dare let this opportunity pass without using it to transform our mistreatment into something good in the lives of others. [Page 139]

If we are distressed, it is for your comfort and salvation; if we are comforted, it is for your comfort, which produces in you patient endurance of the same sufferings we suffer.

2 Corinthians 1:6

Discussion Questions

1. Before now, have you thought that your mistreatment was an "opportunity to influence others by the example of your response"? Do you think it is now? Explain.

2. What reason did Paul give in 2 Corinthians 1:6 for his own distress? How was this a therapeutic outlook?

3. What did Paul think being comforted would produce in the Corinthians? How might this happen?

4. Does the phrase "patient endurance" sound passive or active to you? Does it sound appealing or unappealing? How can you recognize it in someone's life?

Chapter Ten: Freedom from the Tyranny of Self

A. When we've suffered hurt, there is tremendous therapeutic value in finding a cause greater than ourselves to which we can commit. If we have no greater cause than seeking our own happiness, we will ultimately become absorbed and obsessed with self. When a self-absorbed person suffers mistreatment, self-pity inevitably follows. We will never be free of the tyranny of the past until we are free of the tyranny of self. [Page 144]

> *Whoever finds his life will lose it, and whoever loses his life for my sake will find it.*

Matthew 10:39

Discussion Questions

1. What does Ron mean by "the tyranny of self"? Have you ever experienced this in your own life? What is it like?

2. Try to think of five people who give of themselves in service to others but who are yet miserable. Is it difficult to come up with such a list? Explain.

3. Rephrase Matthew 10:39 in your own words. What was Jesus saying?

4. Commit yourself for just one week to doing some act of service for another person. Keep a diary and record your outlook on life both before and after your chosen course of action is complete.

B. Because you have been to the desert of mistreatment, you have received a great gift. You now have the gift of empathy. You know what it is like to be mistreated. That gives you the right and the authority to talk to others who have been deeply hurt by life. You have a depth of understanding and insight that few others have. By using your experience of mistreatment instead of simply trying to escape it, you can find the truest form of emotional wholeness and freedom. You can witness the miraculous transformation of hurt into healing. [Page 147]

> *Praise be to the God and Father of our Lord Jesus Christ, the Father of compassion and the God of all comfort, who comforts us in all our troubles, so that we can comfort those in any trouble with the comfort we ourselves have received from God.*

> 2 Corinthians 1:3-4

> *Remember . . . those who are mistreated as if you yourselves were suffering.*

> Hebrews 13:3

Discussion Questions

1. What is the difference between "using" your experience of mistreatment and trying to "escape" it? Which have you been doing?

2. According to 2 Corinthians 1:3-4, why does God comfort us in our troubles?

3. What does it mean to "remember . . . those who are mistreated"? In what way are we to remember them? How would you like to be "remembered"?

4. Do you see your trial of mistreatment as a "great

gift"? Do you believe your trial has made you empathetic? Explain.

C.   There is a place beyond mistreatment, and that place is in eternity. When you arrive at that place, you will be able to look back on all the evil events in your life and there will be no more pain in those memories. For then, at last, you will be able to see the complete design. You will see how the pattern of your hurt has been interwoven with the pattern of all those millions of others who have suffered unjustly.

And then you will understand. [Page 152]

I consider that our present sufferings are not worth comparing with the glory that will be revealed in us. The creation waits in eager expectation for the sons of God to be revealed. . . . We know that the whole creation has been groaning as in the pains of childbirth right up to the present time. Not only so, but we ourselves, who have the firstfruits of the Spirit, groan inwardly as we wait eagerly for our adoption as sons, the redemption of our bodies. For in this hope we were saved. But hope that is seen is no hope at all. Who hopes for what he already has? But if we hope for what we do not yet have, we wait for it patiently.

Romans 8:18-19, 22-25

Let us fix our eyes on Jesus, the author and perfecter of our faith, who for the joy set before him endured the cross, scorning its shame, and sat down at the right hand of the throne of God. Consider him who endured such opposition from sinful men, so that you will not grow weary and lose heart.

Hebrews 12:2-3

Discussion Questions

1. What keeps the ideas in *Mistreated* from being mere "pie in the sky in the great by-and-by"?

2. How could the thoughts contained in Romans 8 help to give the apostle Paul a positive outlook on life? To what great hope did the apostle look forward?

3. According to Hebrews 12:2-3, how did Jesus manage to endure the cross? Why does the writer mention this fact?

4. What ultimate hope do you have? Describe it. How does this hope help you to persevere in the present? Take some time to thank God for revealing "the end of the story" to his children, and ask him to continue supplying you with his strength.

Acknowledgments

A number of my friends have contributed significantly to the development of this book. My friend and brother in Christ, Jim Denney, has tirelessly edited, researched, developed, and refined the material contained within this work. His efforts are obvious on every page and there would have been no book without him.

Helen McKinney, my administrative assistant and my friend, has carefully critiqued each chapter of this book and has constantly been an encouragement to Jim Denney, to our friends at Multnomah Press, and to me. Helen is a special gift given by God's grace to assist me in my ministry.

Two outstanding Christian psychologists, Dr. Tom Granata and Dr. James Osterhaus, have added their insights and suggestions to sections of this book. Each has also served as friend to aid me in my own lifelong journey toward wholeness in Christ.

Further appreciation must be expressed to my new friend, Steve Halliday, editor for Multnomah Press. He has given in a sacrificial way of his time and creativity to enhance this work. Joan Callahan, a very special sister in Christ, has spent many hours organizing various materials and illustrations from my messages so that I could more readily adapt their insights into this volume.

I must acknowledge loving appreciation for my family. My wife, Shirley, and our children, Rachael and Nathan, have been a special support and encouragement to me throughout the months of study and preparation of the message in this book.

Finally, I am thankful to the scores of friends who have courageously permitted me to share the stories of their trials with you. Their transparency and vulnerability for the sake of others have given this book a dimension of realism and practicality that would otherwise have been impossible to achieve.